A BASKET
BY THE DOOR

About Sophie

Born and raised in Sydney, now living with her family on their farm just outside Orange in country New South Wales, Sophie Hansen trained in journalism and has over 20 years' experience as a features writer. She has contributed to *Australian Country Style* and *Outback* magazines; she was an editor for Slow Food International's English website, lived in Italy for 3 years and is fluent in Italian. In 2013 she set up her blog, *Local is Lovely*, and her podcast, *My Open Kitchen*, is going into its third season. Sophie has been awarded Australian Rural Woman of the Year in recognition of her commitment to rural communities. She believes in simple, tasty and seasonal food, made with love and shared generously.

Instagram: @locallovely @myopenkitchen

A BASKET
BY THE DOOR

Sophie Hansen

MURDOCH BOOKS
SYDNEY · LONDON

Contents

Food for thought

Cooking for another – be it a full meal or a jar of biscuits – is the most thoughtful act of all. It shows someone that you care enough to set aside Sunday morning to make a chicken pie for them. That you care about their wellbeing. And that, however tired, sad or sick they might feel, someone is watching out for them.

I didn't fully understand this concept until I met and fell for a farmer, shortly thereafter moving to the country and my new home, our family farm about half an hour out of Orange, New South Wales. Thirteen years later, I have been on the giving and receiving end of many a care package and have seen firsthand how this generosity can make a difference in the best and worst of times – when babies are born or bushfires threaten, in loss or in illness.

The day Tim and I brought our eldest, Alice, home from hospital, there was a basket by the door. It contained a bottle of wine, an apple cake and a tray of lamb shanks ready to be reheated and, as it turned out, eaten that night, one-handed, bewildered by and besotted with the tiny creature that created this seismic shift in our lives.

There are many things I appreciated about that token of friendship. Firstly, that the giver didn't drop it off when we were home, come in for tea and stay for an hour. I know this doesn't sound very welcoming, but when you are just out of hospital and feeling less than shiny, unexpected visitors can be more stressful than beneficial. Secondly, I appreciated the wondrous fact that dinner was sorted for the next two days. And that someone cared enough to make, pack and deliver these things to our door, well out of town. It was a gesture I'll never forget and a care package that inspired me to write.

Divided into seasons, this book contains over 140 recipes woven into menus and scenarios to cover some of life's big moments. Some of these call for a basket by the door: a new baby, illness, or a friend recovering from surgery, heartbreak, diagnosis or disappointment. And, while I know that a basket of food will never fix everything or anything, it might at least bring the knowledge that someone wants to help. And on a practical level, it means there's a good, gentle meal at the ready: food that is designed to nourish, bolster or cheer.

At the other end of the spectrum, there are joyful menus for gatherings of your nearest and dearest – excuses to come together for comforting kitchen suppers, picnics, camping expeditions, celebrations and small daily wins. And because I think the best present is a pantry stocked with home-made jams, chutneys, cordials and fruit butters, there are menus and ideas for these too.

Most of the recipes can (and should) be doubled. The idea is that while you are lovingly baking for a friend, you are also putting dinner or afternoon tea in the fridge or pantry for yourself. A classic win–win.

This is a heartfelt, home-made book. I took the photos over a year at our table, on our farm and my parents' property, at both special and prosaic moments. Every recipe is simple, tasty and seasonal, because while fancy food can be fun, wholehearted food is what we truly crave when life gets tricky. A crumble with custard, a golden chicken pie, a freshly baked chocolate cake: food that doubles as a hug.

Some of the recipes are quick and easy, some take a little more time. While I know we are all really busy, I hope that this book inspires you to dedicate the odd Sunday morning to cooking good things, not only for your own family but another family too. Throw open the windows, enlist helpers, play your favourite music and take pleasure in the process as much as the end result. Smelling, tasting and being, dare I say it, in the moment.

I hope you enjoy my book and that you find within its pages some ideas and inspiration to leave a basket by someone's door soon.

Sophie x

A confession...

Don't judge, but if you leave something in my car or house, you will probably never see it again. Take the basket in our hallway, for example. It's full of bucket hats, swimming goggles, drink bottles, Tupperware lids and the like. Unless named, I have no idea who they belong to. Even if they are named, I think I'll put things in the kids' school bags to give back, but in the early morning madness, it never happens. So I'm really sorry to anyone who has items sitting in the black hole that is our 'lost property basket'.

Am I the only hopeless non-returner? I suspect not. While people will always be incredibly thankful for any gift of food, don't expect them to return the vessel it came in, especially if your friend is going through tough times. So lower your expectations and instead of gifting a casserole or cake in your expensive new dish, maybe use an old pre-loved container or make your own wrapping.

I have a basket where I hide all my nice paper, pens, material scraps, tape and other bits and pieces for wrapping and labelling food. The kids think it's full of boring stuff so they never open it up to pilfer. You can wrap cakes in muslin or beautiful naturally dyed linen and tie them with twine; or in baking paper, and then tightly in brown paper. Give biscuits or nuts in a glass jar tied with ribbon. Take inspiration from the Japanese art of furokushi and use scraps of fabric to wrap and tie anything from loaves of bread to ugly plastic containers into gorgeous home-made gifts.

Practical tips for giving food

Remember some general rules of thumb, so the care packages you make and give your loved ones don't make them (or you) sick. Always wash your hands before cooking and be aware of safe temperatures and storage times. Once cooked, cool food on the bench until the steam stops rising, then place it in the fridge; don't let food cool completely on the bench. And don't put hot food in the freezer: cool it in the fridge first. Cooked food can generally be safely stored in the fridge for 3–4 days only.

To freeze casseroles, divide into servings of a size that suit your family, place in freezer-safe containers or bags, label with the date and dish's name and freeze for 2–3 months. Avoid freezer burn by using good thick resealable plastic bags or quality

containers, and leave a couple of centimetres at the top of the bag or container to allow the food to expand when frozen. The best and safest place to thaw frozen food is the fridge. Always transport food packed in a cool box or in an insulated bag surrounded with plenty of ice packs or bricks.

Beeswax food wraps

These wraps have become popular in recent years as a smart, eco-friendly alternative to plastic wrap. And while you can find them in shops, beeswax wraps are usually fairly expensive. But here's the good news: they're super-cheap and easy to make. So grab some fabric (an old shirt or pillowcase) and make up a bunch of wraps to give away as presents and/or wrap gifts, sandwiches for school lunches, cover bowls of leftovers and so on.

You'll need 200 g (7 oz) solid beeswax (find it online or in speciality stores), 1 tablespoon olive oil, pinking shears, an old paintbrush, baking paper, a few baking trays and 6–8 fabric rectangles (they'll need to fit on your baking trays, so use that as a size guide).

Preheat the oven to 150°C (300°F). Line your baking trays with baking paper and place a piece of fabric on each. Melt the beeswax in a glass bowl over a pan of simmering water, stir in the oil, then brush it over the fabric. Pop in the oven for a few minutes, then brush again so the wax evenly and lightly covers the fabric. Hang on a clothesline to dry and they're ready to use. Wash beeswax wraps in lukewarm water, never in the dishwasher! If you find them a bit stiff, just work with your hands for a minute until the warmth makes them pliable.

Watercolour gift tags

I'm not at all arty but I have recently, thanks to my artist mum, Annie Herron, started to play around with little line drawings coloured in with a blush of watercolour paint. If you start small and slow, anyone can draw and paint, even a tiny bit.

After spending most of my days at a computer or racing around, I love pulling out my watercolours after dinner to paint little labels for preserves, salts and other gifts. Have a try – it's a very unscary way to be creative.

Spring

Spring nourish basket

Coconut and lemongrass broth with zucchini 'noodles' ~ Pistachio, cardamom and rose balls
Bright and zingy green smoothie ~ Strawberry, almond and cardamom smoothie ~ Fresh almond milk

I would have loved to find this basket of goodies on arriving home from
hospital with a newborn. In fact, I'm sure anyone needing a little gentle nourishment
would be delighted to receive it. The noodle broth provides a soothing, healthy dinner,
while the smoothies and bliss balls will sort out any hunger pangs. For an even
more perfect package, add a bag of Granola (page 33) and a parcel of
Brunekager biscuits (page 107).

Coconut and lemongrass broth with zucchini 'noodles'

COCONUT AND LEMONGRASS BROTH WITH ZUCCHINI 'NOODLES'

This simple, super-tasty broth is an excellent marriage of comfort and zing, the creamy coconut milk bringing the former and the zippy aromatics the latter. It's also great for those trendy 'soup jar' situations that are all over Pinterest and an excellent 'not-sad desk lunch' (see page 156).

1 bunch coriander (cilantro)
4 lemongrass stems
2 x 400 ml (14 fl oz) tins coconut milk
4 cm (1½ inch) piece ginger, peeled and finely chopped
2 French shallots, finely diced
1 bird's eye chilli, halved lengthways
1 tsp palm sugar (jaggery)
8 kaffir lime leaves
Juice of 3 limes, plus extra lime wedges to serve
2 Tbsp tamari or soy sauce
2 zucchini (courgettes)
100 g (3½ oz) vermicelli noodles, cooked according to packet instructions
1 handful greens (shredded kale, roughly chopped English spinach, bok choy, etc.)

Chop off the coriander roots and rinse off any grit. Toss the stalks in the compost or chook bin and reserve the leaves. Trim the tops and bottoms off the lemongrass stems and bruise each stem with the flat side of your knife to release as much of the beautiful flavour as possible.

Pour the coconut milk into a saucepan and add the coriander roots, lemongrass, ginger, shallots, chilli and palm sugar. Crush the lime leaves in your palm to release the flavour, and add to the pan. Bring to a gentle boil, then reduce the heat to low and simmer for 25 minutes.

Strain the broth and discard the aromatics. Stir in 1 cup (250 ml) water, the lime juice and tamari. Check the flavour – you want a good balance of sweet, sour and salty.

To prepare the zucchini noodles, if you have a spiraliser, now is the time to drag it out of the back of the cupboard. Otherwise a julienne peeler or a regular sharp knife will do the job nicely.

If serving immediately, pour the hot coconut broth over the zucchini and vermicelli noodles and throw a few of the greens into each bowl. Serve with the reserved coriander leaves and an extra squeeze of lime.

To prepare for later, pour the coconut broth into a thermos or jar and place the noodles and greens in another container. To serve, reheat the broth if necessary and pour it over the noodles and greens.

SERVES 2

This makes an easy lunch or dinner for a friend in need of TLC.

PISTACHIO, CARDAMOM AND ROSE BALLS

'Bliss balls' and the like are super popular these days, and for good reason – they are filling, delicious, easy to make and last well. And while some can be a bit dense and rubbery, these fragrant little numbers are neither. You could swap the LSA mix with almond meal and leave off the chocolate if you're being a bit more health conscious.

½ cup (70 g) pistachios
½ cup (60 g) LSA mix
8 dates, pitted
1 Tbsp honey
1 tsp vanilla bean paste
1 tsp rosewater
¼ tsp ground toasted cardamom (page 130)
A generous pinch of sea salt, plus extra to serve
½ cup (75 g) roughly chopped white chocolate
Edible flowers, to garnish (optional)

Combine all the ingredients (except the chocolate and flowers) in a food processor or high-powered blender. Blend to a rough, sticky paste.

With damp hands, roll the mixture into 10 to 12 balls about the size of a walnut shell. Pop in the fridge to cool and firm up for at least 15 minutes.

Melt the white chocolate in a bowl over a saucepan of simmering water. Drizzle the chocolate over each ball, sprinkle with a few edible flowers and a little more sea salt and return to the fridge for the chocolate to set.

MAKES 10–12

BRIGHT AND ZINGY GREEN SMOOTHIE

1 small handful kale or English spinach
1 ripe banana (preferably frozen)
1 kiwifruit, peeled
1/2 avocado, stone removed
3 dates, pitted
3 or 4 mint leaves
1 Tbsp chia seeds
1 cup (250 ml) coconut water or plant milk of your choice
Juice of 1 lime
A few ice cubes

Mix all the ingredients in a high-powered blender until smooth.

SERVES 1

We often forget about breakfast when sending and giving food to friends, but when you're feeling a bit fragile or exhausted, having something nutritious, easy and filling ready to go is an enormous help. When you're tied up with a new baby or recovering from an illness or operation, you don't always have the ingredients or time to put them together. These smoothies will keep in the fridge for up to 2 days. Just give them a good shake before drinking, and keep them cool while transporting. See page 92 for some more tasty smoothie ideas.

I liked it & my youngest was excited to make it but didn't love it in the end.

STRAWBERRY, ALMOND AND CARDAMOM SMOOTHIE

6 large strawberries
1/4 tsp ground toasted cardamom (page 130)
1 tsp grated fresh ginger
3 dates, pitted
A pinch of sea salt
1 cup (250 ml) fresh almond milk (see recipe, right) or store-bought
A few ice cubes
Honey, to taste

Mix all the ingredients in a high-powered blender until smooth. Sweeten to taste with a little honey (although I find if the strawberries are nice and sweet you don't need to).

NOTE
You could make this creamy smoothie with regular milk or any other nut milk, but I do especially love it with freshly made almond milk.

SERVES 1

FRESH ALMOND MILK

Soak 1 cup (160 g) raw almonds overnight in cold water. Drain and tip into a high-powered blender along with 1 cup (250 ml) water and a pinch of sea salt and blitz for 30 seconds or until you have a smooth paste. Add 2 cups (500 ml) water and 2 pitted dates and blitz for 1 minute. Grab a piece of muslin (or a nut milk bag) and drape it over a large sieve. Pour the almond milk through the sieve and squeeze out as much liquid as possible. Store the milk in the fridge for a couple of days. Give it a shake before using. You can use the left-over almond pulp in muesli or bread dough, or feed it to your chooks like I do.

Smoothies are wonderful — they pack loads of goodness into one glass.

Gifts from the garden

Beetroot, walnut and pomegranate dip ~ Spiced broad bean and pea dip
Quick pickled baby vegetables ~ Bread and butter pickles ~ Seedy lavosh

This little collection is packed with perfect spring colours, plus loads of flavour.
Easy to transport, eat and keep, any of these dips or pickles would make a beautiful
package with a jar full of seedy crackers. Remember to double the recipes so that
you can also fill your own fridge and pantry shelves.

BEETROOT, WALNUT AND POMEGRANATE DIP

This dip is great with pickled or fresh vegetables and crackers, served alongside barbecued meats, used as a base for a quinoa salad bowl or spread across toasted sourdough and topped with a little feta and rocket (arugula).

4 beetroot (about 700 g/1 lb 9 oz), trimmed
1 Tbsp olive oil, plus extra for drizzling
1 cup (115 g) walnuts, toasted
1 handful dill
Grated zest and juice of 1 lemon
2 Tbsp pomegranate molasses, or to taste
1/2 tsp sea salt and a good grinding of black pepper, or to taste
1/4 cup (70 g) Greek-style yoghurt

Preheat the oven to 180°C (350°F). Cut the beetroot into quarters, place on a baking tray and drizzle with a little olive oil. Roast for 35 minutes, then tip the walnuts onto another baking tray and add them to the oven for 10 minutes or until they're just turning golden and smelling lovely and aromatic, at which point remove them from the oven. Check that the beetroot is cooked (it'll be tender right through when pierced with a knife) and remove it from the oven as well.

Put the beetroot and walnuts in the bowl of a food processor and add the dill, lemon zest, lemon juice, 1 tablespoon olive oil, pomegranate molasses, salt and pepper. Blitz until you have a smooth-ish purée, then add the yoghurt a little at a time until the dip reaches the desired consistency. Season to taste before serving.

MAKES ABOUT 2 1/2 CUPS

SPICED BROAD BEAN AND PEA DIP

A deliciously chunky, green dip that's excellent served with crackers and pickles or alongside some grilled fish or chicken. You could also purée this until smooth, thin it out with a nice stock and serve as soup.

2 cups (350 g) broad beans
1 cup (140 g frozen or 160 g fresh) green peas
1 handful coriander (cilantro) leaves
1 handful mint leaves
1 red chilli, finely chopped, or to taste
1/4 tsp sea salt
A good pinch of ground cumin
Grated zest and juice of 1 lime
2 Tbsp Greek-style yoghurt

Blanch the broad beans and peas in boiling water for a few minutes, then drain and refresh under cold water. Double-pod the broad beans if you have time (nobody will really mind if they're only single-podded – the extra step just makes the dip a little smoother and brighter).

Transfer the broad beans and peas to the bowl of a food processor and add the remaining ingredients. Blitz until the dip has a rough consistency. Season to taste, and serve with fresh and/or pickled vegetables and crackers.

MAKES ABOUT 1 1/4 CUPS

Make a double quantity to keep in the fridge for emergency snacking.

QUICK PICKLED BABY VEGETABLES

These are also known as 'fridge pickles' or 'the lazy person's pickle', because you don't need to worry about sterilising jars and the like. They are intended to be consumed within a couple of weeks, so they're an easy way to get a little more mileage out of your garden or market haul. Milder and less vinegary than regular pickles, these are especially good made with sweet, pretty baby vegetables. Serve them with dips or a cheese platter, or use them to pep up a simple grain salad.

*Enough raw vegetables to fill four
  2 cup (500 ml) jars (see Note)*
*2 cups (500 ml) vinegar (I use 2 parts
  apple cider vinegar and 1 part white
  wine vinegar)*
¼ cup (55 g) sugar
2 Tbsp sea salt
1 Tbsp coriander seeds, toasted
1 Tbsp yellow mustard seeds
1 Tbsp black peppercorns
1 tsp chilli flakes
1 tsp fennel seeds

Trim your vegetables, slicing any large ones, then pack tightly and prettily into four large jars.

Pour 1½ cups (375 ml) water into a small saucepan and add the vinegar, sugar, salt and spices. Bring to the boil over medium heat.

Carefully pour the hot liquid into the jars, ensuring that the vegetables are completely covered. Seal well and leave on the bench to cool, then store in the fridge for 2–3 weeks. Wait for a day or two before eating the pickles as this will allow the flavours to develop.

MAKES 4 JARS

NOTE
Use any vegetables you like – baby carrots, radishes, beetroot, fennel, green beans, garlic scapes, turnips, zucchini (courgettes), etc. If using cucumber, keep in mind that it has a high water content, so I'd reduce the water by at least ½ cup (125 ml).

BREAD AND BUTTER PICKLES

This recipe is from my mother-in-law, Judith, who enjoys making pickles and delivering them to friends. We are always happy to see lines of pickle jars on her kitchen bench, waiting for us to take home to pile on cheese sandwiches or add to mezze platters with toasted flatbread, yoghurt, olives, tomatoes and feta. Judith adds these pickles to peanut butter sandwiches and serves them alongside barbecued meats, especially our venison.

8 baby Lebanese cucumbers, cut into 6 mm
   (1/4 inch) slices
2 red onions, thinly sliced
2 tsp salt
1 3/4 cups (435 ml) white wine vinegar
1 cup (220 g) sugar
2 tsp brown mustard seeds
1 tsp fennel seeds
1 tsp coriander seeds

Combine the cucumber, onion and salt in a small bowl and toss well to combine. Cover and place in the fridge overnight (this will soften the cucumber before pickling). The next morning, rinse the cucumber and onion slices and pat dry.

Combine the vinegar, sugar and spices in a small saucepan. Cook over medium heat for 5 minutes, stirring often to dissolve the sugar. Add the sliced cucumber and onion and bring to the boil. Remove from the heat, divide among sterilised jars and seal well. Wait for a couple of days for the flavours to develop before cracking the pickles open.

MAKES ABOUT 3 CUPS

SEEDY LAVOSH

This simple recipe produces gorgeously crisp, flavoursome crackers that are excellent with dips or cheeses. Make up a jar to deliver to a friend, and also keep some in your pantry for snacking at any time of day.

1 1/3 cups (200 g) plain flour
1/3 cup (50 g) sesame seeds
1 tsp fennel seeds
1 tsp nigella seeds
1 tsp sea salt, plus extra for sprinkling
1/4 cup (60 ml) olive oil, plus extra for brushing

Preheat the oven to 170°C (340°F). Grease and line a baking tray with baking paper.

Mix together the flour, seeds and salt in a large bowl. Whisk the olive oil and 1/2 cup (125 ml) water in a small jug, stir into the dry ingredients and work into a rough dough. Turn out onto a work surface and gently knead until soft. Divide the dough into four or five pieces. Roll out one piece of dough between two sheets of baking paper until about 2 mm (1/16 inch) thick. Transfer to the baking tray, brush with a little olive oil and sprinkle with sea salt. Bake the lavosh for 15 minutes or until golden brown, then set aside to cool. Repeat with the remaining dough.

Break the cooled lavosh sheets into shards and store in an airtight container. Alternatively, you can cut the lavosh into neater squares before baking.

VARIATIONS
Instead of (or as well as) the seeds, you could add 1 teaspoon finely chopped fresh or dried rosemary or oregano. A few chilli flakes worked through the dough before baking are good, too.

MAKES ABOUT 20 PIECES

A breakfast picnic is a lovely
friendly way to start the day.

Bring on breakfast

Wholemeal orange and almond muffins ~ Rhubarb compote
Roasted oranges with rosemary and vanilla
Light and crunchy honey granola ~ Spiced coffee

Breakfast often gets overlooked when you're unwell, busy or too stressed to think about anything other than getting well or getting sorted. I'm a big fan of giving someone a basket of breakfast provisions as a gesture of how much you care. It also offers a practical solution to a problem they probably haven't even conceived of yet: that having nothing decent at home for breakfast leads to 'hangriness' (i.e. the angry hunger feelings) by about 11am. In my experience, the 11am hangry pangs tend to lead to bad eating decisions, which lead to feeling even worse and guilty, and so the cycle continues.

Make and pack up these goodies to leave by someone's door or, better yet, organise a breakfast picnic in the golden light of early morning. It's a lovely, friendly way to start the day – and by 9am you've had a good catch-up and you still have the rest of the day ahead of you.

WHOLEMEAL ORANGE AND ALMOND MUFFINS

I'm not usually much of a muffin person. They're often too big, cake-y and sugary for me. But these breakfast muffins are something else entirely – full of flavour and just the right amount of sweetness. Thanks to the roasted almond meal, they stay moist and fresh for longer than a regular muffin. They're delicious served with Rhubarb compote (see below) and a little Greek-style yoghurt.

1 cup (150 g) wholemeal plain flour
1/2 cup (50 g) almond meal (using freshly roasted, ground almonds makes all the difference)
1/2 cup (110 g) caster sugar
1/4 cup (45 g) soft brown sugar
1 1/2 tsp baking powder
1 egg
150 g (5 oz) butter, melted
100 g (3 1/2 oz) natural Greek-style yoghurt
1 tsp vanilla bean paste
2 oranges, peeled and cut into small chunks

Preheat the oven to 200°C (400°F). Line a 12-hole standard muffin tin with paper cases.

Combine the flour, almond meal, sugars and baking powder in a bowl. Whisk the egg, butter, yoghurt and vanilla together, then gently fold into the dry ingredients until just combined (take care not to over-mix). Fold in the oranges or any extra flavourings (see Variations).

Divide the batter among the muffin cases and bake for 20 minutes or until the muffins are golden on top and firm to touch.

VARIATIONS
Add 1/2 cup (85 g) chocolate chips and use hazelnut meal instead of almond meal.
Use 1 cup (220 g) poached and roughly chopped pear or quince instead of the oranges.
Replace the oranges with 1 cup (150 g) fresh berries.

MAKES 12

RHUBARB COMPOTE

Preheat the oven to 180°C (350°F). Slice 1 bunch (300 g/10 1/2 oz) trimmed rhubarb into 3 cm (1 1/4 inch) batons and place in a small roasting tin lined with baking paper. Split 1 vanilla bean lengthways and add it to the tin with the juice of 2 oranges and 1/3 cup (75 g) caster sugar. Toss well, then cover with foil and roast for 25 minutes or until the rhubarb has completely collapsed. **Makes about 2 cups**

ROASTED ORANGES WITH ROSEMARY
AND VANILLA

These roasted oranges are superb with granola and some Greek-style yoghurt. One of my lovely recipe testers commented on the delicious smell that filled the kitchen when she was cooking. Rosemary and citrus are an excellent match, and together make for a comforting, cheerful-smelling kitchen.

4 oranges, *peeled and sliced into thick rounds*
1/3 cup (75 g) caster sugar
1 rosemary sprig
1 vanilla bean, split lengthways

Preheat the oven to 180°C (350°F). Line a roasting tin with foil, then top with a sheet of baking paper. Put the oranges on the paper and add the sugar and rosemary. Scrape the vanilla seeds over the oranges and add the vanilla bean. Toss to combine, then wrap up into a tight parcel.

If making this to enjoy now, roast for 25 minutes or until the oranges are soft and fragrant. If making this as a gift, tie the parcel with some twine and add a tag with the cooking instructions.

SERVES 4 (WITH GRANOLA)

good but not great for all the work did make alot of great candied orange peels though

LIGHT AND CRUNCHY HONEY GRANOLA

A lovely big bag of home-made granola is one of the best things you can give anyone. It is, of course, wonderful for breakfast, but it's also good sprinkled over yoghurt and a bit of fruit at any time of day. This recipe is based on a version I enjoyed one winter morning in Canberra at the very cool cafe, Mocan and Green Grout. It was served in a beautiful bowl with warm roasted rhubarb, topped with yoghurt and shards of black sesame praline. You can add the rhubarb and praline if you like, but I also love it with yoghurt and warm Roasted oranges with rosemary and vanilla (see opposite).

½ cup (175 g) honey (orange blossom is good here)
Grated zest of 1 orange
1 tsp vanilla bean paste
2 cups (40 g) puffed millet or puffed brown rice
2 cups (200 g) rolled oats
1 cup (160 g) almonds, roughly chopped
1 cup (155 g) hazelnuts, skinned and roughly chopped
1 tsp toasted ground cinnamon
½ tsp ground ginger
A pinch of ground coriander
A pinch of ground cardamom
A pinch of ground cloves
½ tsp sea salt

Preheat the oven to 150°C (300°F). Line two large baking trays with baking paper.

Gently warm the honey in a small saucepan over medium–low heat until runny. Stir in the orange zest and vanilla. Combine the remaining ingredients in a large bowl, then stir in the warm honey mixture.

Spread the granola over the trays and cook for 40–50 minutes, turning and tossing the mixture and swapping the trays every 10 minutes until golden. Turn off the oven and leave the granola in there to cool – this helps it become crunchy. Store the granola in an airtight container for up to a couple of weeks.

MAKES 5 CUPS

burned!

SPICED COFFEE

Combine 2 cups (175 g) freshly ground coffee (for a plunger) with 2 Tbsp soft brown sugar, ½ tsp ground toasted cardamom (page 130) and ½ tsp ground ginger in a large heatproof jug. Split ½ vanilla bean lengthways and add it to the jug, scraping in the seeds. Pour in 3 cups (750 ml) boiling water and leave to infuse overnight.

Line a sieve with four layers of muslin (or a couple of clean Chux cloths) and place over a large bowl. Pour the coffee mixture into the sieve and discard the coffee grounds. Store the coffee concentrate in the fridge.

To serve, heat the coffee concentrate in a small saucepan, then mix 1 part concentrate with 1 part boiling water (or to taste) and add milk (to taste). **Makes 3 cups (750 ml) concentrate**

Hit the couch

Fennel and sausage ragu ~ Spicy, smoky beef ragu
Just a really good chocolate mousse ~ Blood orange margaritas

These recipes are for when you or your recipient are too sad to do anything more than
sit on the couch, eat something comforting and watch something distracting.
At times like these you need carbs, sausages, a stiff drink, chocolate and
a good line-up of movies or TV shows. I offer up two different but
equally delicious slow-cooked ragu recipes here – take your pick.

Fennel and sausage ragu

FENNEL AND SAUSAGE RAGU

This ragu is all about coaxing the flavour from every ingredient through long, slow cooking. The result is a super-tasty rich sauce to serve over polenta, gnocchi or any kind of pasta. I also use it in my lasagne. If you are making the ragu to give away, bundle it up with some nice pasta, a block of parmesan cheese and a bread stick or, even better, the Garlic bread from page 215.

1/3 cup (80 ml) olive oil
1 red onion, diced
3 garlic cloves, finely chopped
1 tsp fennel seeds
500 g (1 lb 2 oz) really nice Italian sausages (about 4 sausages – a mixture of pork and veal if possible)
200 g (7 oz) pancetta, roughly chopped
1 cup (250 ml) full-bodied red wine
2 x 400 g (14 oz) tins whole tomatoes
1/4 cup (60 g) tomato paste (concentrated purée)
1 cup (250 ml) chicken or vegetable stock

Preheat the oven to 150°C (300°F). Heat the olive oil in a deep ovenproof frying pan or flameproof casserole dish over medium heat. Cook the onion for 5 minutes or until soft and translucent. Add the garlic and fennel seeds and cook for a couple more minutes. Crumble the sausage meat into the pan, discarding the casings. Add the pancetta and increase the heat to medium–high. Cook, stirring often, until the sausage meat and pancetta are browned. Pour in the red wine and let the liquid reduce a little. Now pour in the tomatoes, tomato paste and stock and stir well. Season with salt and pepper to taste.

Clean the side of the pan (any residue may burn and be tricky to wash away). Place in the oven and cook, uncovered, for 3 hours (give it a stir a couple of times). By this point the ragu will have reduced right down.

SERVES 4

SPICY, SMOKY BEEF RAGU

This ragu is layer upon layer of flavour, cooked long and slow in a low oven. It freezes really well and would be great to give someone for a ready meal. I love it with soft polenta and a green salad, but it would also be good with potato mash or even guacamole, tortillas and some pickles.

1/3 cup (80 ml) olive oil
2 onions, finely chopped
4 garlic cloves, finely chopped
1 tsp thyme leaves
2 chorizo sausages, very finely chopped (I give them a whizz in the food processor)
800 g (1 lb 12 oz) chuck steak or other slow-cooking cut, cut into small pieces (your butcher should be happy to do this, otherwise use beef mince)
1 cup (250 ml) full-bodied red wine
2 x 400 g (14 oz) tins whole tomatoes
1/3 cup (90 g) tomato paste (concentrated purée)
4 chipotle chillies in adobo sauce, roughly chopped (you can usually find these in the Mexican section of the supermarket)
1 Tbsp soft brown sugar
1 Tbsp balsamic vinegar
1 tsp salt

Preheat the oven to 140°C (275°F). Heat the oil in a large heavy-based ovenproof saucepan or flameproof casserole dish over medium heat. Add the onion, garlic and thyme and cook, stirring occasionally, for about 10 minutes or until softened.

Add the chorizo, increase the heat to high and cook for a few minutes. Next add the beef and cook for a few more minutes. Pour in the wine and let it bubble down and reduce a little. Add the tomatoes, tomato paste, chillies, sugar, vinegar and salt and stir well.

Transfer to the oven for 4 hours, by which time it will be a rich, deeply flavoured pot of goodness. Stir the ragu every now and then during cooking so that it doesn't stick to the bottom of the pan.

SERVES 6-8

Soooo tasty – wait till it cools even if it smells amazing – lip burns

JUST A REALLY GOOD CHOCOLATE MOUSSE

I'm of the belief that a good chocolate mousse can bring a smile to almost any face. So, if you arrive on the doorstep of a sad friend with a bowl of mousse and two spoons, I am fairly confident that the gesture at least will make him or her smile.

This recipe is inspired by a dessert I enjoyed in Paris with my friends Cook and Sasha. We were travelling on a tiny budget, giddy with the fact that we were in Paris and having dinner in a picture-perfect bistro. I will never forget the chocolate mousse that arrived in a huge bowl with three spoons and a jug of cold cream.

The recipe isn't tricky but it does create rather a lot of washing up. The good news is that it's all done well in advance and hopefully forgotten once you start eating. It doubles really well, so why not make two big bowls of mousse – one for your fridge and one for a friend? Transport it in an cool box or chiller bag and store it in the fridge for up to 3 days.

100 g (3½ oz) good-quality milk
  chocolate
100 g (3½ oz) good-quality dark
  chocolate
3 eggs, separated
½ cup (125 ml) single (pure) cream

If you have an old-school handheld electric beater, now's the time to dig it out. Otherwise, grab an electric mixer with a whisk attachment.

Melt the milk chocolate and dark chocolate together in a glass or ceramic bowl over a saucepan of simmering water, stirring regularly until smooth.

Meanwhile, whisk the egg yolks until pale and fluffy. In another bowl, whip the cream until soft and thick. And in yet another bowl (sorry!), whisk the egg whites until stiff peaks form.

Fold the melted chocolate, a little at a time, into the egg yolks, then fold in the cream and whisk together until smooth (I use a handheld electric mixer here for a quick burst to ensure everything is really well combined). Now very, very gently, fold in the egg whites, a little at a time, until just incorporated. You want to keep as many air bubbles as possible so don't worry if there are still a few streaks of white – I think that's a decent trade-off for such a light mousse. Spoon the mousse into one big bowl or individual glasses and chill for at least 3 hours or for up to 3 days.

SERVES 6

okay, but not going to become a fixture in our home

SUGAR SYRUP

Combine ½ cup (110 g) caster sugar and 1 cup (250 ml) water in a small saucepan. Bring to a simmer and cook, stirring, until the sugar has dissolved. Remove from the heat and set aside to cool. Store in the fridge, ready to use in Blood orange margaritas (see right).
Makes about 1 cup

Cut 1 lime in half, then rub the rims of two glasses with the lime halves. Press the glasses into Lime chilli salt (page 133) or sea salt flakes to coat. Squeeze the lime halves and pour the juice into a cocktail shaker or a jar with 1/2 cup (125 ml) fresh blood orange juice, 1/3 cup (80 ml) sugar syrup, or to taste (see left), 1/3 cup (80 ml) tequila and 1/4 cup (60 ml) Grand Marnier or Cointreau. Add 1 cup (150 g) crushed ice and shake for a good 10 seconds. Pour into the glasses and serve. **Serves 2**

Bring in the big guns

THE chicken pie ~ Syrup-soaked lemon, blueberry and rosemary cake

Drop off a basket containing these goodies and, while it won't unbreak what's broken,
it will at least mean that your friend has a gentle, delicious meal at the ready.
And they'll know that you poured love into it – surely that will part the clouds a little?

THE CHICKEN PIE

I make this pretty much every time I go to cook for someone in need of cheering up. There's something about a golden chicken pie that makes everyone feel good – kids love it, adults do too and it's a whole meal in one.

Yes, this is a labour of love. Yes, you could buy a roast chook and frozen pastry and bung this together in less than half the time and nobody would care. But... there really is something deeply satisfying about making this chicken pie from scratch. And if you do, please take my advice and triple this recipe to make three at once – one to give away, one for your dinner and one for the freezer.

Poaching a whole chicken in aromatics means not only do you get lovely moist chicken and stock to use for the filling and sauce base, but you'll have some chicken and stock left over for sandwiches and soup. Have I convinced you yet?

BASICALLY THERE ARE FOUR PARTS TO THIS PIE:

1. Poach the chicken for chicken meat and stock – 15 minutes hands-on preparation, 1 hour hands-off cooking. (You could substitute a barbecued chicken.)

2. Make the rough puff pastry – 15 minutes hands-on preparation, 50 minutes chilling. (You could use frozen puff pastry instead.)

3. Make the filling – 20 minutes hands-on preparation, 15 minutes cooking.

4. Roll out the pastry, add the filling, assemble and bake – 20 minutes hands-on preparation, 40 minutes cooking.

You don't have to do all of this in one hit. I usually poach the chook and make the filling the day before so it's nice and cool when I put it all together. Then I make the pastry and bake the pie the day I want to deliver or eat it.

One last thing before you get started: I recommend baking this pie in a disposable aluminium pie tin. Not all that beautiful, I know, but they work a treat and mean that your recipient doesn't have to think about washing and returning a dish, which, when you are in need of cheering up, is a bit of a drag.

SERVES 6–8

PART 1:
THE POACHED CHICKEN

1.8 kg (4 lb) whole chicken
2 carrots, roughly chopped
2 celery stalks, roughly chopped
1 onion, roughly chopped
1 tsp black peppercorns
1 tsp sea salt
1 handful parsley (stems and all)
4 thyme sprigs

Wash the chicken and pat dry, then place in a large stockpot, cover with cold water and add the remaining ingredients. Bring to the boil over medium–high heat, watching out for and discarding any scum that comes to the surface (there's a life lesson hidden in a recipe). Reduce the heat and gently simmer for 45 minutes.

Transfer the cooked chicken to a board resting on a tea towel (this will stop any juices dripping onto the bench and the floor). Cover the chicken with a tent of foil and set aside until cool enough to handle.

Return the stockpot to the stovetop and boil until the mixture reduces by about a third – this will take 20 minutes or so and will intensify the flavour. Pour the mixture through a sieve, discarding the aromatics and reserving the stock.

Pull the chicken meat away from the bones and discard the carcass. Cover until needed for the filling or place in the fridge if you're not assembling and baking your pie right away.

PART 2:
THE PASTRY

Rough puff pastry
250 g (9 oz) chilled butter, cut into cubes
1²/₃ cups (250 g) plain flour, plus extra for dusting
¼ cup (60 ml) chilled water

Combine the butter and flour on the bench, using the heel of your hand to work them together. Add water as necessary to form a rough dough – it's okay to see some marbled streaks of butter. Cover with plastic wrap and chill in the fridge for 30 minutes.

On a lightly floured work surface, roll out the pastry until you have a large rectangle. Dust off any loose flour. Fold the top half of the pastry down, then fold the bottom half up so you have a long slim rectangle. Now turn the pastry 90 degrees and roll into another large rectangle, trying to roll in only one direction if possible (this helps keep the butter's 'marbled' effect and ideally will keep your pastry nice and puffy and flaky). Fold and roll again, then cover with plastic wrap and chill for 20 minutes or until needed.

NOTE
If you're using store-bought pastry, I'd recommend shortcrust for the base and puff for the top.

PART 3:
THE FILLING

50 g (1¾ oz) butter
2 leeks, pale parts only, thinly sliced
2 Tbsp plain flour
2 cups (500 ml) hot chicken stock
1 tsp wholegrain mustard
1 tsp lemon thyme leaves
Grated zest of 1 lemon
150 ml (5 fl oz) single (pure) cream
450 g (3 cups) cooked, shredded chicken

Heat the butter in a large frying pan over medium heat until bubbling. Add the leek, season and cook, stirring often, for 10 minutes. Add the flour and cook, stirring, for a couple of minutes.

Add the hot stock and let it bubble for 2 minutes, stirring often, then stir in the mustard, lemon thyme, lemon zest and cream. Bring back to the boil and cook, stirring often, for a few minutes more, until the sauce thickens up. Taste and season again if needed.

Pop the mixture into the fridge to cool while you roll out the pastry and line the pie tin. When you're ready to assemble the pie, stir in the shredded chicken.

NOTE

It's important that the chicken is only reheated once after it's cooked. If you're making this as a helpful present, assemble the pie but don't bake it – just include a note with the baking instructions.

PART 4:
BRINGING IT ALL TOGETHER

1 egg
1 Tbsp single (pure) cream

Preheat the oven to 200°C (400°F). Make an egg wash by whisking the egg and cream together.

Roll out the pastry on a lightly floured work surface to a large round, about 3 mm (⅛ inch) thick. Trim the excess pastry, leaving enough to hang over the side of the pie tin, then gently drape the pastry over your rolling pin and unroll it into a pie tin – mine is 22 cm (8½ inches) wide and 4 cm (1½ inches) deep. Press the pastry into the side of the tin, then run the rolling pin over the top to create a clean edge. Roll the excess pastry into a ball and roll it out to a round slightly larger than the top of your pie tin. Cut a small hole in the middle of the pastry (to let steam escape while cooking).

Spoon the chicken filling into the pie tin, brush the pastry edges with a little egg wash and gently press the pastry lid on top. Pop the pie in the fridge for 5 minutes while you do one last (optional) step. Roll out any pastry remains and use some little cutters or a small sharp knife to cut small triangles or whatever pastry shapes you like. Use these shapes to decorate the edge of your pie and cover up any rough bits.

Brush the pastry top with egg wash. Finally, place the pie in the oven and bake for 35–40 minutes or until the pastry is golden brown. Well done, you!

A really great pie can't put the world to rights, but it might at least part the clouds of unhappiness a little.

SYRUP-SOAKED LEMON, BLUEBERRY AND ROSEMARY CAKE

Nothing tricky or fancy here – just the most lovely, simple and soft cake ever. There's something very comforting in its softness and lemony tang. It freezes well, too. One more cheering attribute of this cake: it's a melt-and-mix number so it's super easy to make.

180 g (6 oz) butter, melted
¾ cup (200 g) plain Greek-style
  yoghurt
Grated zest of 1 lemon
¼ cup (60 ml) lemon juice
3 eggs, at room temperature
2 cups (300 g) plain flour
1½ cups (330 g) caster sugar
2 tsp baking powder
1 punnet (125 g) blueberries
Rosemary sprigs and flowers,
  to garnish (optional)

Rosemary lemon syrup
½ cup (110 g) caster sugar
Grated zest of 2 lemons
¼ cup (60 ml) lemon juice
2 rosemary sprigs

Preheat the oven to 180°C (350°F). Grease a 24 cm (9½ inch) spring-form cake tin or a bundt tin.

Combine all the ingredients except the blueberries in a food processor or large bowl and either whizz for 10 seconds or stir well by hand until you have a smooth batter. Gently fold in the blueberries.

Pour the batter into the tin and bake for 45 minutes or until the cake is golden brown and just firm to touch. While the cake is baking, prepare the syrup.

For the syrup, combine all the ingredients and ¼ cup (60 ml) water in a small saucepan. Bring to the boil, then let the mixture bubble away for a few minutes until you have a thick syrup.

As soon as you remove the cake from the oven, poke it all over with a skewer and pour the hot syrup onto the cake. The holes from the skewer will allow the syrup to penetrate right into the cake. Garnish with rosemary sprigs and flowers if you have them.

SERVES 8

This syrup-soaked cake looks very pretty sprinkled with rosemary sprigs and flowers.

Two lovely tarts for lunch

Filo, spinach and dill tart ~ Hot-smoked salmon and zucchini tart
Radish and pomegranate salad

Springtime here in Orange means lots of eggs, lots of new greens, and picnic season.
And one of the best things to take and share on a picnic, or give to someone as
an instant meal, is a home-made tart. Plan on delivering these the day you make
them, or freeze them and deliver straight into your friend's freezer or
into their fridge to defrost for lunch or dinner.

FILO, SPINACH AND DILL TART

This simple and easy tart can take all kinds of variations. You could swap silverbeet or kale for the spinach, and add a little cooked chicken or smoked salmon to the ricotta mixture.

¼ cup (60 ml) olive oil
1 red onion, finely diced
8 handfuls English spinach (about 1 big bunch), roughly chopped, stalks discarded
A few pinches of salt
1 cup (230 g) ricotta cheese
½ cup (65 g) crumbled feta cheese
4 eggs
Grated zest of 1 lemon
1 handful dill, finely chopped
100 g (3½ oz) butter, melted
6 sheets filo pastry
⅔ cup (100 g) pine nuts, toasted
¼ cup (40 g) sesame seeds

Preheat the oven to 220°C (425°F). Heat the olive oil in a frying pan over medium heat and cook the onion for 5 minutes or until soft. Add the spinach, a handful at a time, waiting for it to wilt a little before adding more. Add a few pinches of salt as you go and cook until all of the spinach has just wilted. Remove from the heat and set aside.

Put the ricotta in a large bowl and whisk in the feta, eggs, lemon zest and dill. Season to taste.

Grease a 24 cm (9½ inch) spring-form cake tin with a little of the melted butter. Lay the pastry out on a work surface. Brush one pastry sheet with the melted butter and gently lay it across the tin, then press into the tin so the excess pastry is hanging over the side. Repeat with the remaining pastry sheets.

Spoon the spinach mixture into the pastry, top with the ricotta mixture and sprinkle with the pine nuts. Bring the pastry edges over the top to make a rough lid. Brush with a little more butter and sprinkle with the sesame seeds. Bake for 35 minutes or until the pastry top is golden brown.

SERVES 6-8

HOT-SMOKED SALMON AND ZUCCHINI TART

Just the loveliest little tart, this one – singing with fresh spring flavour. Once you've prepared the pastry base, it's easy to put together – winning all round!

1 quantity rough puff pastry (page 40)
2 eggs
½ cup (125 ml) single (pure) cream
½ cup (50 g) finely grated parmesan cheese
Grated zest of 1 lemon
300 g (10½ oz) hot-smoked salmon, flaked
1 zucchini (courgette), very thinly sliced

Roll out the pastry on a lightly floured surface until about 5 mm (¼ inch) thick. Drape the pastry over the rolling pin and unroll it into a loose-based fluted tart tin – mine is 20 cm (8 inches) wide and 3 cm (1¼ inches) deep. The pastry will shrink back into the tin when cooking, so minimise this by leaving extra at the top and really pushing the pastry down and into each indent in the side of the tin. Trim the edge, leaving about 5 mm (¼ inch) extra. Return to the fridge for 30 minutes.

Preheat the oven to 200°C (400°F). Prick the pastry base with the tines of a fork. Line with baking paper and fill the base with pastry weights, uncooked rice or dried beans (this stops the base rising during baking). Bake for 10 minutes, then gently remove the weights and baking paper and cook for another 5–10 minutes or until the pastry is just lightly golden and looks dry. Meanwhile, prepare the tart filling.

Whisk together the eggs and cream. Season to taste, then add half of the parmesan and the lemon zest. Pour into the pastry and add the salmon and zucchini. Sprinkle with the remaining parmesan and grind some black pepper over the top. Bake for 25–30 minutes or until the top is golden and just firm to touch.

VARIATIONS
Instead of the zucchini and salmon, you could also use asparagus and goat's curd; caramelised onion and thyme; or roasted pumpkin and beetroot.

SERVES 6-8

The crunchy radish salad works particularly well to offset the rich, creamy salmon tart.

RADISH AND POMEGRANATE SALAD

Cut one telegraph cucumber into chunks, slice a bunch of radishes into thin discs and pick the leaves off a bunch of mint. Combine in a large bowl. Dress with a simple lemon and olive oil dressing and sprinkle with some nigella seeds and pomegranate seeds.
Serves 6

Golden syrup biscuits

An afternoon tea basket

Jam pastries ~ Golden syrup biscuits ~ Vietnamese iced coffee ~ Dot's sponge

This is the kind of afternoon tea basket that will keep helpers
happy on a working bee, bring a sweet note to a tricky gathering
or just make someone feel extra loved and looked after.

JAM PASTRIES

Few home-made treats are more appreciated than a batch of warm pastries filled with jam or vanilla custard. They do, I concede, require terrifying amounts of butter, but... needs must! Fill them with jam as I've done here, or with custard, a layer of frangipane and some thin slices of poached pear or apple. Or try apple and custard, sprinkled with some slivered almonds. Fresh berries are also delicious.

The pastries are best on the day they're made, but can be reheated the next day. If you're freezing them, pop them in the oven straight from the freezer to reheat.

1 Tbsp (15 g) dried yeast
150 ml (5 fl oz) lukewarm water
A pinch of salt
2 Tbsp caster sugar, plus extra
    for sprinkling
1 egg
350 g (2⅓ cups) plain flour, plus
    extra for dusting
320 g (11¼ oz) chilled unsalted
    butter, cut into thin strips
½ cup (165 g) jam (quince is
    particularly good)

Egg wash
1 egg
2 Tbsp single (pure) cream

Mix the yeast with the water. Add the salt, sugar and egg and, using your hand shaped like a claw, bring everything together into a lovely shaggy mess. Add the flour and turn the mixture out onto a lightly floured surface. Knead until smooth and elastic, about 5 minutes. Place the dough in a lightly oiled bowl, cover with plastic wrap and leave it to rest in the fridge for 30 minutes.

Roll out the dough on a lightly floured surface into a large rectangle, about 40 x 30 cm (16 x 12 inches). Arrange all of the butter in the centre. (I know it looks like a lot, and it is, but it's worth it.) Fold the dough edges over the butter to meet in the middle, as if you're making a dough envelope.

Turn the dough over so the seam is sitting underneath, then gently roll into a 40 x 30 cm (16 x 12 inch) rectangle again. Fold a third of the dough into the centre, then fold the other third over the top so that you have three layers of dough. Wrap in plastic and pop back in the fridge for 20 minutes. Take out, reroll and return to the fridge for another 20 minutes. Repeat the rolling and chilling once more.

Line a large baking tray with baking paper. Gently roll out the pastry into a 48 x 36 cm (19 x 4¼ inch) rectangle and cut this into 12 cm (4½ inch) squares. Place a dollop of jam in the centre of one pastry square, fold the edges over to make a little parcel and place on the tray. Repeat with the remaining pastry squares. Let the pastries rest in a warm place for 20 minutes. Meanwhile, preheat the oven to 220°C (425°F).

Whisk the egg and cream together to make an egg wash. Brush over the pastries, sprinkle with a little extra sugar and bake for 15 minutes or until golden brown.

MAKES 12

GOLDEN SYRUP BISCUITS

When I make these biscuits, I feel happy and loved. The taste and smell catapult me back to my Gran's old kitchen in the Blue Mountains. I hope you find them as deliciously comforting as I do.

200 g (7 oz) unsalted butter, softened
1 cup (220 g) caster sugar
2 Tbsp golden syrup
1 tsp vanilla bean paste
2 cups (300 g) plain flour
1 tsp baking powder
A pinch of salt

Preheat the oven to 180°C (350°F). Grease and line two baking trays with baking paper.

Using an electric mixer with a paddle attachment (or a wooden spoon and a strong arm), cream the butter, sugar, golden syrup and vanilla until pale and fluffy.

Sift the flour, baking powder and salt together, then add to the butter mixture. Tip the mixture out onto a work surface and bring together until just combined.

Split the dough into six balls. Roll and squeeze each ball into a sausage shape, about a thumb's width and around 16 cm (6¼ inches) long. Place on the baking trays and bake for 15 minutes or until golden and slightly risen. They will flatten and spread out quite a bit – don't worry! Remove from the oven and cool for a few minutes before cutting into biscuits about 4 cm (1½ inches) wide.

MAKES ABOUT 30

VIETNAMESE ICED COFFEE

Combine 1 cup (250 ml) strong filter coffee, 1 cup (135 g) ice cubes and 1 Tbsp sweetened condensed milk in a large jar. Screw the lid on tightly and give everything a good shake. Serve immediately or shake again before serving. **Serves 2**

DOT'S SPONGE

The best sponge ever! Fluffy, light and just so delicious – big thanks to Dot Yeatman and the team at the Manildra flour mill in central western New South Wales for this recipe.

This cake is bound to cheer and please. Make it for your favourite birthday person, a work afternoon tea, or to enter in your local show. I've doubled Dot's recipe to make a nice tall layer cake, but if you'd prefer something a little smaller or just one layer, then halve away.

8 eggs, separated
1½ cups (330 g) caster sugar
⅔ cup (100 g) self-raising flour
1 cup (125 g) cornflour
1 cup (250 ml) Lemon and passionfruit curd (page 244)
300 ml (10½ fl oz) single (pure) cream, whipped
250 g (9 oz) strawberries, sliced
4 passionfruit

Preheat the oven to 180°C (350°F). Grease and line two 20 cm (8 inch) spring-form cake tins with baking paper.

Whisk the egg whites to a stiff froth. Gradually add the sugar and beat until thick and smooth. Whisk in the egg yolks, one at a time. Sift the flours together three times. Fold into the egg and sugar mixture with an upward and over movement (do not stir).

Pour half the batter into each cake tin and bake for 20–25 minutes or until the cakes are just firm to touch. Set aside for 5 minutes before turning out onto a wire rack to cool.

Spread the lemon curd over one cake and top with some of the whipped cream, then top with the second cake. Decorate with the remaining cream, strawberries and passionfruit pulp.

MAKES ONE 20 CM (8 INCH) CAKE

Spring picnic hamper

Caramelised onion butter ~ Chicken sandwich mix with a wholegrain loaf
Garlic scape and zucchini fritters ~ Swirly, crunchy rocky road

Spring is the perfect time for country picnics. The snakes aren't awake yet
(or shouldn't be), the flies aren't out in force yet (or shouldn't be) and it's not too
hot to throw out a rug and spend an afternoon with friends, feasting in the sun.
This menu makes a really lovely spring picnic but it could just as easily be
packaged up and given to a lucky friend.

Caramelised onion butter with radishes

CARAMELISED ONION BUTTER

I adore this richly flavoured butter. It's delicious with fresh, peppery radishes, but also pretty special served with a perfectly barbecued steak or stuffed into a roast potato and topped with chives and/or rocket (arugula) leaves.

¼ cup (60 ml) olive oil
3 onions, diced
1 tsp fennel seeds
150 g (5½ oz) unsalted butter, softened
Smoked sea salt, to taste (see Note)

Heat the oil in a frying pan over medium–low heat, add the onion and cook for 15 minutes or until soft and caramelised. Transfer the onion to a bowl to cool.

Wipe out the frying pan and toss in the fennel seeds, then return to the heat and toast for a few minutes or until fragrant. Add the fennel seeds to the bowl with the onion.

Once the onion has cooled, add the butter and salt and stir until well combined. Pack the butter into a bowl or roll it into a log, wrap in baking paper and place in the fridge to firm up.

NOTE
Smoked sea salt is easy to find in most delicatessens. You could, of course, just use regular sea salt and it would still be delicious – the smoked version just adds a little extra oomph.

MAKES ABOUT ½ CUP

Double this recipe and keep a batch in the freezer for flavour emergencies.

CHICKEN SANDWICH MIX WITH A WHOLEGRAIN LOAF

Chicken sandwiches make a simple but very tasty picnic lunch, and they are also great for school lunches. You can either make up the sandwiches or present them in parts as I have done here – the mix and the sliced bread can be frozen. Take care to keep the chicken mixture cool while in transit – a cool box or chiller bag and an ice brick will do the trick.

Many friends have also told me that chicken sandwiches stand out as the most useful, tasty offering they have been gifted during difficult times. One friend told me that after her father passed away, a neighbour came around with a tray of tightly wrapped chicken sandwiches and put them straight in the freezer. A few nights later, the family, completely exhausted after the funeral, collapsed on the couch with a few beers and the thawed chicken sandwiches. She said it was one of the most welcome meals of her life.

Shredded meat from 1 whole poached chicken or purchased barbecued chicken (see Note)
¾ cup (185 g) good-quality mayonnaise
½ cup (80 g) pine nuts, toasted
3 celery stalks, diced
1 handful dill, finely chopped
Juice of 1 lemon
2 Tbsp dijon mustard
1–2 loaves fresh, sliced wholegrain bread

Mix the shredded chicken with the mayonnaise, pine nuts, celery, dill, lemon juice and mustard. Season to taste. Serve with the sliced bread.

NOTE
You'll need about 3 cups (450 g) of shredded cooked chicken. I like to poach a whole chicken following the instructions in the chicken pie recipe (page 40) – this is cheaper and yields more delicious chicken, but there's nothing wrong with using a barbecued chook.

MAKES ABOUT 8 SANDWICHES OR 24 FINGER SANDWICHES

GARLIC SCAPE AND ZUCCHINI FRITTERS

Garlic scapes appear in our farmers' markets in spring, right before the garlic harvest. They are long, curly shoots with a punchy, peppery garlic flavour. They're gorgeous stir-fried, pounded into pesto or sliced and fried up in these tasty little fritters. These are ideal picnic or basket fare, great at room temperature or straight from the pan. If you can't lay your hands on garlic scapes, spring onions mixed with a couple of finely chopped garlic cloves would work beautifully too.

3 zucchini (courgettes), grated
½ tsp salt
1 bunch garlic scapes (about 8), trimmed
    and finely chopped
½ cup (115 g) ricotta cheese
2 eggs
1 tsp grated lemon zest
¾ cup (110 g) self-raising flour
Olive oil, for frying

Minted yoghurt
1 cup (260 g) plain yoghurt
1 handful mint leaves, finely chopped
Juice of 1 lemon
Chilli flakes (optional)

Combine the grated zucchini and salt in a small bowl. Transfer the mixture to a colander and set it above the bowl. Leave to drain for 30 minutes.

Meanwhile, for the minted yoghurt, mix the yoghurt, mint and lemon juice together. Season to taste, and top with a few chilli flakes if you like it hot. Cover and chill while you prepare the fritters.

Combine the drained zucchini with the garlic scapes, ricotta, eggs and lemon zest in a bowl and mix well. Fold in the flour and season to taste.

Heat a tablespoon or so of olive oil in a frying pan over medium–high heat. Dollop a tablespoon of the batter into the pan and then add two more dollops so you are cooking three fritters at once, for about a minute on each side or until golden brown. Transfer to a plate lined with paper towel. Repeat with the remaining batter, then serve warm or at room temperature with the minted yoghurt.

MAKES ABOUT 12–15

delicious, but I have to remember that
I can't 'fry' things in my
current kitchen.

SWIRLY, CRUNCHY ROCKY ROAD

Rocky road always goes down well and this one, I promise, will be a particular crowd pleaser. I love the salted peanuts, and the ginger works well for me, but you can of course swap in or out anything you prefer. Try adding half a cup of broken shortbread biscuits, or perhaps some jellies or dried cranberries.

1⅓ cups (200 g) roughly chopped good-quality
    dark chocolate
1⅓ cups (200 g) roughly chopped good-quality
    white chocolate
1 cup (90 g) nice marshmallows, cut into pieces
    with scissors
¾ cup (110 g) salted peanuts
½ cup (110 g) crystallised ginger
Edible flowers, to decorate

Grease and line a 20 cm (8 inch) square cake tin with baking paper. Melt the dark chocolate in a bowl over a saucepan of simmering water. Do the same with the white chocolate, in a separate bowl.

Stir the marshmallows, peanuts and ginger into the dark chocolate. Spoon the mixture into the tin and swirl in the white chocolate, using a knife to mix. Sprinkle with a few edible flowers for decoration, then place in the fridge to set for at least 2 hours.

Once hardened, cut the rocky road into pieces and package up for your lucky friends. If the weather's warm, store it in the fridge.

MAKES ABOUT 20 PIECES

Spring drinks to bottle

St Joseph's lemonade ~ Elderflower cordial ~ Elderflower vodka ~ Strawberry and elderflower pops

I like to prepare ahead for the Christmas season and stock the pantry with
beautiful bottles of home-made drinks. It means I always have something
a bit special at the ready, either to give as a gift or to enjoy with friends.

ST JOSEPH'S LEMONADE

This recipe comes via St Joseph's school in Molong, New South Wales. The kids there made a big batch of lemonade to sell and raise funds for their kitchen garden, which I visited and wrote about for my blog. It's a great simple recipe and extra easy when you have lots of little hands to help squeeze all those lemons!

800 ml (28 fl oz) freshly squeezed
   lemon juice
Zest of 2 lemons (slice thin strips
   of the skin, so it is easy to
   remove later)
2 kg (4 lb 8 oz) sugar
3 tsp citric acid

Pour 2.4 litres (84 fl oz) water into a large saucepan. Add the lemon juice and lemon zest and bring to the boil. Pour in the sugar, stirring until it has dissolved. Take the pan off the heat and stir in the citric acid. Allow to cool, then discard the lemon zest.

Strain the lemon juice and divide among sterilised bottles. Seal and store in the fridge.

MAKES 4 LITRES OR JUST OVER FIVE 3 CUP (750 ML) BOTTLES

Dilute the lemonade mix with cold water and serve with lots of ice.

ELDERFLOWER CORDIAL

20 elderflower heads
4 lemons
2¼ cups (500 g) caster sugar

Wash the elderflower well. Juice one of the lemons; thinly slice the rest.

Combine the sugar and 4 cups (1 litre) water in a large non-reactive saucepan and bring to the boil, stirring until the sugar has dissolved. Remove the pan from the heat. Add the lemon juice, lemon slices and elderflower. Cover the pan and set aside for 24 hours.

Strain the liquid, discarding the flowers and lemon slices. Decant the cordial into sterilised jars ready to be given away or stored in your fridge.

MAKES 4 CUPS (1 LITRE)

There's something quite special about the creamy, lemony, floral aroma of elderflower. It grows wild along the creek on our farm and seems to pop up along roadsides and in gardens all over the country. Apparently one must endeavour to pick elderflower only on sunny days, only picking the flower heads that are facing the sun. Or so they say.

I love elderflower cordial with lots of sparkling water and ice, but it's also gorgeous with prosecco or vodka and soda, and makes a lovely jelly or sorbet base. The elderflower vodka is also lovely with sparkling water over crushed ice.

ELDERFLOWER VODKA

10 elderflower heads
1 cup (220 g) sugar
Grated zest and juice of 1 lemon
4 cups (1 litre) vodka

Pick through the flowers to make sure there aren't any bugs or other nasties in there, then pack them into a large jar. Add the sugar, lemon zest, lemon juice and vodka, then seal and give it a good shake. Leave in a dark place to infuse for one month.

Line a strainer with muslin and strain the vodka into a clean bottle. The vodka will be delicious to drink now, but will develop a more full-bodied flavour after a month or two.

MAKES 4 CUPS (1 LITRE)

STRAWBERRY AND ELDERFLOWER POPS

Blend 250 g (9 oz) strawberries with 1 cup (250 ml) elderflower cordial and 2 cups (500 ml) water. Check the taste. The flavour will dull a little when frozen, so you might want to make it sweeter than you would make it to drink by adding more cordial. If it's too sweet, add a little more water or puréed strawberries. Pour into 8 ice-block moulds (if you don't have them, ice-cube trays will do the trick). Freeze for at least 4 hours or until frozen solid. **Makes 8**

Sweet pickles parcel

Sweet verjus-pickled rhubarb with bay ~ Sweet verjus-pickled strawberries with vanilla and pink peppercorns
Orange and quinoa biscuits

These sweet pickles make a lovely care package for a friend in need of a bit of extra love. Sweet pickles are a gorgeous way to semi-preserve soft spring berries and such. These recipes are 'fresh pickles', meaning they aren't made to last for months, just a week or so, and need to be kept in the fridge. They are beautiful served with goat's curd and the not-too-sweet orange and quinoa biscuits, but also fantastic with harder, stronger cheeses or even over ice cream or a simple almond cake or cheesecake. Verjus is the perfect pickling agent to use here. The acid is softer than vinegar or lemon juice, yet enough to cut through the fruit's sweetness.

SWEET VERJUS-PICKLED RHUBARB WITH BAY

1 bunch or 300 g (10½ oz) trimmed rhubarb,
  cut into 2 cm (¾ inch) pieces
¾ cup (185 ml) verjus
½ cup (110 g) caster sugar
1 vanilla bean, split lengthways
Zest of 1 lemon, cut into thick strips
3 bay leaves

Pack the rhubarb into a large jar. Combine ½ cup (125 ml) water with the verjus, sugar, vanilla bean, lemon zest and bay leaves in a small saucepan. Bring to the boil, stirring occasionally, then remove from the heat and set aside to cool for 10 minutes.

Pour the mixture over the rhubarb, seal and store in the fridge for up to a week.

MAKES 1 LARGE JAR

SWEET VERJUS-PICKLED STRAWBERRIES WITH VANILLA AND PINK PEPPERCORNS

500 g (1 lb 2 oz) strawberries,
  hulled and halved
¾ cup (185 ml) verjus
½ cup (110 g) caster sugar
1 vanilla bean, split lengthways
Zest of 1 orange, cut into thick strips
1 tsp pink peppercorns

Pack the strawberries into a large jar. Combine ½ cup (125 ml) water with the verjus, sugar, vanilla bean, orange zest and pink peppercorns in a small saucepan. Bring to the boil, stirring occasionally, then remove from the heat and set aside to cool for 10 minutes.

Pour the mixture over the strawberries, seal and store in the fridge for up to a week.

MAKES 1 LARGE JAR

ORANGE AND QUINOA BISCUITS

Dead easy to make, these taste beautiful and pack loads of crunch. Plus, they last for ages in the biscuit tin and are perfect spread with goat's curd and topped with either of the sweet pickle concoctions. They also make a great base for ice cream sandwiches.

50 g (1¾ oz) butter, melted
1⅓ cups (125 g) quinoa flakes
1 cup (220 g) caster sugar
2 eggs, lightly beaten
2 Tbsp plain flour
2 tsp baking powder
A pinch of salt
Grated zest of 1 orange

Preheat the oven to 180°C (350°F). Line two baking trays with baking paper.

Mix the melted butter with the quinoa flakes, sugar and eggs. Sift in the flour, baking powder and salt, add the orange zest and gently mix together.

Drop small amounts of the mixture onto the trays (about a teaspoon for each biscuit). Leave plenty of space for the mixture to spread – at least 5 cm (2 inches) between each one. (I usually make only six biscuits per tray.) Bake for 12 minutes or until golden. Leave on the tray to cool for a few minutes before transferring to a wire rack to cool completely.

MAKES ABOUT 20

Chilly spring evening supper

Baked ricotta with spring greens ~ Nutty sweet potato and lime soup

Spring can mess with your head and wardrobe, don't you think? Just when I think it's warming up and put away the warm blankets and woollies, the weather turns cool again. This basket of goodness is for those chilly spring nights. Get a few friends together, set the kitchen bench with a jar of pretty spring flowers and catch up over a bowl of soup and a beautiful baked ricotta. Or pack this up and deliver it to someone in need of some soothing soup and a friend. Add the Triple-ginger loaf from page 164 for extra brownie points.

BAKED RICOTTA WITH SPRING GREENS

Baked ricotta is something I make constantly, always the same basic recipe, topped with whatever might be in season or just baked as it is. It's beautiful served warm or at room temperature, in wedges or small cubes with drinks, even sliced and sandwiched between warm slices of sourdough toast. It's also great to make and give away as it keeps quite nicely for a few days and makes a change from the good old frittata.

2 cups (460 g) ricotta cheese
1 cup (95 g) grated parmesan cheese, plus extra
   for sprinkling
5 eggs (lovely big free-range ones)
1 tsp thyme leaves
2 handfuls spring greens – I've used broad beans,
   baby leeks sliced into thin strips, some roughly
   chopped new season garlic and a few chopped
   asparagus spears

Preheat the oven to 180°C (350°F). Grease and line a cake tin, roughly 28 x 22 cm (11¼ x 8½ inches), with baking paper (or grease well).

Whisk the ricotta, parmesan, eggs and thyme, and season with salt and pepper.

Spoon the mixture into the tin. Top with the spring greens and a little extra parmesan, then pop into the oven for about 25 minutes or until golden brown and just firm to touch. Serve warm or at room temperature. Lovely with a good home-made chutney.

SERVES 4–6

Brian & I enjoyed but Scotty hated the texture and Holden was like okay.

NUTTY SWEET POTATO AND LIME SOUP

With the soothing heft of sweet potato and a lighter note thanks to the lime and lime leaves, this is a gorgeous soup and just the thing for a cool spring dinner.

2 Tbsp extra virgin olive oil
1 brown onion, finely diced
750 g (1 lb 10 oz) sweet potato, peeled
   and cut into 4 cm (1½ inch) chunks
4 cm (1½ inch) piece ginger, peeled and
   roughly chopped
2½ cups (625 ml) chicken or vegetable stock
6–8 kaffir lime leaves
⅓ cup (90 g) nice natural peanut butter
1 tsp soft brown sugar
Juice of 2 limes, plus extra to serve
1 cup (250 ml) coconut milk

Heat the olive oil in a large saucepan over medium–high heat. Cook the onion for a few minutes until soft and translucent. Add the sweet potato and ginger and cook for a few more minutes, then pour in the stock and bring to the boil.

Scrunch the lime leaves in your palm to release the flavour, then add to the pan and reduce the heat to a simmer. Cook for about 20 minutes or until the sweet potato is tender. Discard the lime leaves.

Blend the soup with the peanut butter and brown sugar until smooth. Stir in the lime juice and enough coconut milk to bring the soup to the desired thickness. Check the seasoning, adding a little more lime juice, salt or a touch of sugar to get that lovely balance of sweet, salty and sour. Serve with extra lime juice.

SERVES 4–6

Not as great as Austin's & where the hell does one find kefir lime leaves

Summer

Italian summer buffet

Vitello tonnato ~ Melon and prosciutto
Amaretti and dark chocolate roasted peaches ~ Cherry frangipane galette

During my late twenties, I called the northwestern Italian province of Piedmont home, and this rather grown-up menu is a catalogue of my Italian favourites from that time. The dishes can all be prepared in advance and served either at room temperature or warmed up, so it can be made ahead and just taken out of the fridge when you're ready. Present it buffet-style, with lots of crusty bread for an excellent Sunday lunch or dinner.

This would also be a great meal to prepare and put in the fridge of a friend who has a large number of people to feed, when it's actually the last thing in the world they feel like doing.

This delicious menu is a catalogue
of my Italian favourites.

VITELLO TONNATO

Vitello tonnato can be found on pretty much every osteria menu across Piedmont. It's a classic dish of poached veal knuckle, thinly sliced and served on a bed of rocket (arugula) under a blanket of tonnato sauce, which is essentially a tuna-spiked mayonnaise (it sounds weird but is truly wonderful). I once visited an osteria in the town of Alba and was served a main dish of one onion, slow cooked for hours so it was a globe of caramelised sweetness, doused in tonnato sauce. It was one of the most memorable meals of my life and so inspiring to see the humble onion served as the star of a main course.

You see how awesome and versatile this sauce is? Make a double batch to serve with everything from onions to roasted capsicums (peppers), grain salads or grilled short-loin lamb chops.

One of the best things about this dish is that it can (and actually should) be made up to 2 days in advance, then covered tightly and left in the fridge for the veal to absorb all the flavours of the sauce. Served with crusty bread, it's a complete meal solution done and dusted in advance.

The dish pictured here was made in Tuscany while I was cooking for one of the art classes my mum, Annie Herron, hosted for a few years. I used the classic veal in this case, but at home I give it a more local twist by using a lightly seared fillet of the venison we produce on our farm.

TONNATO SAUCE

1/2 cup (120 g) home-made or best-quality mayonnaise
185 g (6 1/2 oz) tin tuna in olive oil
4 anchovy fillets, drained
2 Tbsp capers, rinsed
Juice of 1 lemon
2 Tbsp olive oil

Put the mayonnaise, tuna (with the oil from the tin), anchovies, capers, lemon juice and olive oil in the bowl of a food processor or blender and blitz until you have a smooth, thick sauce. Check the flavour and add more lemon juice or salt and pepper to taste.

Store in a jar or covered container in the fridge for up to a week.

VARIATION
Make the tonnato sauce thicker by using a little less mayonnaise and serve it as a dip or spread. It's really yummy spread on sourdough with a slice of tomato and some chilli flakes – something I happen to be eating as I write this and nodding in enthusiasm for its deliciousness!

good!

MELON AND PROSCIUTTO

The combination of cool, sweet rockmelon and salty, chewy prosciutto is an established summer staple in Italy, and perfection on a hot summer day. A plate of this with another of rocket (arugula), a few warm ripe tomatoes, a ball of fresh mozzarella cheese and some good olive oil with a bottle of chilled rosé for lunch is up there with my best meals ever. And it takes all of 5 minutes to throw together. All you do is find a nice firm rockmelon, cut it into wedges, remove the skin and wrap each wedge with a piece of prosciutto. Keep it in the fridge until serving time.

POACHED VEAL

2 Tbsp olive oil
1–1.3 kg (2 lb 4 oz–3 lb) veal nut
1 onion, roughly chopped
2 carrots, roughly chopped
2 celery stalks, roughly chopped
A few cloves, bay leaves and juniper berries
1 cup (250 ml) white wine

Heat the oil in a large flameproof casserole dish over high heat and sear the veal all over for a few minutes on each side. Remove from the pan and set aside.

Add the vegetables and aromatics to the pan and cook over medium heat for 5 minutes. Pour in the wine and let it bubble, stirring often, for a minute or so. Return the veal to the pan and pour in 3 cups (750 ml) water (or enough to just cover the meat). Bring to the boil, then reduce the heat to a simmer. Cook the veal for 15 minutes (it will feel firm but a little springy), then remove it from the liquid and set aside to cool.

The poaching liquid can be turned into a lovely, rich veal stock. To do this, put the pan over high heat until reduced by at least half (it will take about 40 minutes). Strain and store in the fridge or freezer to use in your next casserole, soup or risotto.

TO SERVE

4 handfuls rocket (arugula)
3 lovely, ripe, room-temperature tomatoes, quartered
4 anchovy fillets
1 Tbsp capers, rinsed
1 Tbsp flat-leaf parsley, roughly chopped
Olive oil, for drizzling
2 lemons, quartered
2 baguettes, sliced

Scatter the rocket across a platter, thinly slice the veal and arrange slices on top of the rocket. Spoon the tonnato sauce over the meat so it covers it fairly generously, but leave the edges uncovered. Tuck in the tomato wedges and sprinkle with the anchovies, capers, parsley and a good drizzle of olive oil. Place a few lemon wedges around the edges and serve with crusty bread.

SERVES 6

AMARETTI AND DARK CHOCOLATE ROASTED PEACHES

I absolutely love serving these peaches for dessert with vanilla ice cream or cream, and they're pretty much the only dish I make or take to dinner parties on hot summer nights. One or two chilled peaches with some Greek-style yoghurt also makes a fabulous breakfast or brunch.

80 g (2¾ oz) unsalted butter, cut into small cubes, plus extra for greasing
6 ripe yellow peaches
6 amaretti biscuits
½ cup (75 g) finely chopped dark chocolate
¼ cup (45 g) soft brown sugar
1 cup (250 ml) rosé or light white wine

Preheat the oven to 180°C (350°F). Rub a large ovenproof dish with a little butter.

Halve the peaches and remove the stones. Using a small, sharp knife, cut into and around the cavity left by each stone to make it a little bigger. Put the peach halves in the dish, cut side up.

Crush the amaretti biscuits into a small bowl. Mix in the chocolate, butter and brown sugar. Divide the mixture among the peach halves, stuffing as much as possible into each cavity. Drizzle with the wine and bake for 35 minutes or until the peaches are soft but haven't completely collapsed.

SERVES 4–6

These peaches are equally good chilled, at room temperature or served hot straight from the oven.

CHERRY FRANGIPANE GALETTE

Three things I love about this tart: you don't need to blind bake it, it almost looks better if the edges are a bit rough, and it travels beautifully. It's one of my favourites and such a gorgeous way to celebrate the short cherry season. If cherries aren't in season, just use peaches, nectarines, figs or any kind of berry instead. Or if it's coming in to autumn, try using poached quinces.

The pastry can be made in a food processor, but I quite like doing it by hand, feeling the flour and butter coming together and taking the time (no more than 5 minutes) to quietly knead it together. Plus, by the time I get my food processor out, find the blade, lid and so on, then make the pastry, clean said parts and put them away, I don't think there's much time difference between the two processes. And the former is definitely more pleasant than the latter.

Sweet shortcrust pastry
200 g (1⅓ cups) plain flour, plus extra for dusting
⅓ cup (40 g) icing sugar
¼ tsp ground cardamom (see page 130 for my ground toasted cardamom)
A pinch of salt
150 g (5½ oz) chilled unsalted butter, cut into small cubes
¼ cup (60 ml) iced water

Frangipane filling
80 g (2¾ oz) butter, softened
½ cup (110 g) caster sugar
¾ cup (80 g) almond meal
1 Tbsp plain flour
1 egg
1 tsp natural vanilla extract

To assemble
3 cups (450 g) pitted cherries
¼ cup (50 g) demerara sugar

To make the pastry, combine the flour, icing sugar, cardamom and salt on a work surface. Bring into a mound and make a well in the centre. Fill the well with the cubed butter and a splash of the iced water. Use the heels of your hands to bring everything together, working the butter into the flour and adding more water as needed. Keep going until you have a rough dough. Shape into a disc, cover with plastic wrap and place in the fridge to rest for 30 minutes.

For the frangipane filling, cream the butter and sugar together until pale and fluffy. Fold in the almond meal, flour, egg and vanilla, mixing until smooth. Keep the frangipane at room temperature if you're using it soon, otherwise place it in the fridge for up to a week, or freeze it.

Preheat the oven to 200°C (400°F). Line a baking tray with baking paper. Lightly dust your work surface with flour, then gently roll out the chilled pastry into a large round, about 3 mm (⅛ inch) thick. Carefully transfer the dough to the tray.

Spread the frangipane mixture over the pastry in a 1.5 cm (⅝ inch) thick layer, leaving a 5 cm (2 inch) border. Arrange the cherries on the frangipane, piling them on top of each other. Bring in the pastry edges, pinching with your fingertips or folding to form little pleats. Sprinkle with the demerara sugar and bake for 25 minutes or until the pastry is golden brown. Serve the galette warm or at room temperature with custard (page 154), ice cream, cream or yoghurt.

NOTE
You may find that the recipe makes more frangipane mixture than you need, but this isn't a bad thing. Roll up any excess in baking paper and freeze it. For a quick dessert, cut some frozen puff pastry into squares, top each with a few slices of frozen frangipane and let it thaw a little. Top with a few slices of peach, a few berries or other seasonal fruit, pinch up the pastry to form an edge and bake until golden.

SERVES 4–6

If I were an organised person,
this menu is what I'd always
pack for long summer car trips.

Playing it cool

Paydirt salad with peaches, tomatoes and mint
Cold soba noodle salad with trout and pickled cucumber ~ Mum's pork and pistachio terrine
Raw chocolate peppermint slice ~ Raw raspberry, orange and cashew slice

If I were an organised person, this is what I'd always pack for long car trips in summer, accompanied by our road trip playlist. I would happily eat the two salads every day of summer. The two slices are nourishing in the sense that they're made from whole, good ingredients that will fill you or your intended recipient with nuts, good fats and good feelings. Even if they're not exactly health food.

PAYDIRT SALAD
WITH PEACHES, TOMATOES AND MINT

Every year, on our way home from holidays, we stop at Paydirt Eatery in Braidwood, New South Wales. This recipe is my interpretation of a lunch I enjoyed there some years ago. I ordered it as a takeaway and it was presented, wrapped in brown paper, with a large purple fig sitting on top. The fig was warm from the sun, freshly picked from the chef's garden. It was such a memorable experience and everything I aim to achieve in my food – generous, thoughtful and tasty, with seasonal produce as the star of the show.

I encourage you to try this bright, crunchy, tangy and sweet summer salad. It's a total winner on its own or served as a side dish to grilled fish or perhaps barbecued chicken thighs marinated first in soy, honey and mirin.

Thank you, Paydirt, for inspiring this, my new favourite salad. It's not quite as good as yours, but it's still pretty delicious.

2 cups (150 g) finely shredded cabbage
2 handfuls mint leaves
1 handful tarragon leaves
1 cup (175 g) chopped cucumber
1 cup (150 g) cherry tomatoes, quartered
3 French shallots, thinly sliced
2 perfectly ripe peaches, thinly sliced
2 Tbsp nigella seeds
1/4 cup (35 g) raw peanuts

Dressing
1/2 cup (125 ml) lime juice
2 Tbsp fish sauce
1 tsp soft brown sugar
1 tsp very finely chopped red chilli, or to taste

Toss together all the salad ingredients.

Mix the dressing ingredients together in a jar, season and adjust to taste. Dress the salad just before serving.

SERVES 4

COLD SOBA NOODLE SALAD WITH TROUT AND PICKLED CUCUMBER

This is perfect for hot summer days or nights when you can't bear the idea of cooking. The flavours are gentle but delicious and the cold slurp of the slippery soba noodles is highly comforting.

400 g (14 oz) soba noodles
1 handful mint leaves
1 handful Thai (or regular) basil
    leaves
½ handful coriander (cilantro) leaves
½ cup (60 g) finely chopped spring
    onions (scallions)
¼ cup (40 g) sesame seeds, toasted
¼ cup (40 g) poppy seeds
300 g (10½ oz) hot-smoked trout

Pickled cucumber
½ cup (125 ml) rice wine vinegar
2 Tbsp sugar
1 long telegraph cucumber, thinly
    sliced
Grated zest and juice of 1 lime

Dressing
¼ cup (60 ml) mirin
¼ cup (60 ml) soy sauce
1 Tbsp rice wine vinegar
1 Tbsp sesame oil
1 Tbsp grated fresh ginger

For the pickled cucumber, combine the rice wine vinegar and sugar in a small saucepan. Bring to a simmer and cook, whisking a little, until the sugar has dissolved. Pour into a bowl and pop in the fridge. Once the mixture is cool, pour it over the cucumber and add the lime zest and juice. Cover and set aside while you get everything else ready.

Whisk the dressing ingredients together, then set aside.

Cook the noodles according to the packet instructions. Drain, then rinse under cold water, working the noodles between your fingers to wash away excess starch. Toss the noodles with the dressing.

When ready to assemble, toss the pickled cucumber, herbs, spring onion and seeds through the noodles. Flake the trout over the salad, give a gentle toss and serve, or return to the fridge until needed.

SERVES 4

MUM'S PORK AND PISTACHIO TERRINE

1 handful sage leaves
1 handful flat-leaf parsley leaves
2 garlic cloves
$1/2$ tsp sea salt
6 black peppercorns
300 g ($10^{1}/_{2}$ oz) pork mince (see Note)
300 g ($10^{1}/_{2}$ oz) beef mince
$1/2$ cup (70 g) pistachios
$1/4$ cup (60 ml) white wine
1 brown onion, finely diced
2 Tbsp olive oil
10 rashers streaky bacon

My mum is a big terrine maker. Her standard picnic basket includes one just like this, along with a bowl of hard-boiled eggs, a loaf of bread, a jar of home-made chutney and some greens.

If you're considering making up a basket of goodies for a family in need of easy meals for tricky days, a terrine is a winner. It can sit in the fridge ready to make into a quick lunch or dinner with a salad, or cut into thick slices for sandwiches, with some chutney.

Combine the sage, parsley, garlic, salt and peppercorns on a chopping board and chop together until fine. In a large bowl, combine the pork and beef mince, the pistachios, wine and herby garlic mixture. Mix together well, then cover and place in the fridge for 1 hour for the flavours to combine.

Meanwhile, put the onion in a frying pan with the olive oil. Cook over medium heat for about 10 minutes or until the onion is completely soft and translucent. Spread out on a tray to cool completely.

Preheat the oven to 160°C (320°F). Line a 30 x 8 cm (12 x $3^{1}/_{4}$ inch) loaf tin with the bacon, placing three strips lengthways along the bottom of the tin and the rest crossways, letting the ends hang over the sides.

Mix the cooled onion into the pork mixture, then press it into the tin. Fold the bacon over the top to make a lid and wrap tightly in foil. Line a roasting tin with a tea towel and place the terrine in the middle (the tea towel stops the terrine from moving around while you're moving the tin in and out of the oven). Place the roasting tin on the middle rack of your oven and carefully pour enough boiling water into the tin so that it reaches about halfway up the sides of the loaf tin.

Bake for $1^{1}/_{2}$ hours, then remove the roasting tin from the oven and let the terrine cool for about 15 minutes in the water bath.

Remove the terrine from the roasting tin. Cover with a sheet of baking paper and weigh down with a few tins of tomatoes or such. Leave the terrine in the fridge overnight or for at least 6 hours. Store in the fridge for 3–4 days.

NOTE
If possible, ask your butcher to roughly mince pork shoulder and a beef chuck cut. Otherwise, regular mince is fine.

SERVES 8-10

RAW CHOCOLATE PEPPERMINT SLICE

The key to this easy slice is the peppermint oil. If you can lay your hands on a proper peppermint essential oil, it will lift the game considerably and transform this into a cooling, completely delightful treat. You should be able to find it at health food shops or online. I have a small bottle that cost me about $40, which I know sounds like a lot but it lasts for ages as you only need a drop or two.

Base
1 cup (160 g) almonds
1 cup (90 g) desiccated coconut
$1/3$ cup (40 g) unsweetened dark cocoa powder
3 Tbsp rapadura sugar, honey or maple syrup
A pinch of sea salt

Middle
3 cups (270 g) desiccated coconut
1 Tbsp coconut oil
2 Tbsp honey or maple syrup
2 drops peppermint essential oil

Top
$1/2$ cup (55 g) unsweetened dark cocoa powder
$1/3$ cup (80 ml) melted coconut oil
2 Tbsp rapadura sugar, honey or maple syrup

Grease and line a 20 cm (8 inch) square cake tin with baking paper. Mix all the base ingredients in a food processor until well combined. Press into the tin and pop in the freezer for 20 minutes.

For the middle layer, clean out the food processor, then add all the ingredients and blitz until well combined. Press the mixture over the base, then return to the freezer to set for another 20 minutes.

For the top layer, mix the ingredients in a small bowl until well combined. Pour over the middle layer and smooth the top. Place in the fridge to set for at least 30 minutes, then cut the slice into squares to serve.

MAKES 18 PIECES

RAW RASPBERRY, ORANGE AND CASHEW SLICE

A pretty and super-delicious slice, this makes a great present and is very easy to put together. Keep it in the freezer and transport in a cool box or chiller bag with an ice pack or it will soften and lose shape. As with the peppermint slice, this is a filling treat, so serve in small squares.

Base
$1^1/2$ cups (225 g) pitted dates
$1/2$ cup (110 g) 'no-sugar' crystallised ginger
3 cups (480 g) almonds
$1/2$ cup (125 g) coconut oil
$1/2$ tsp sea salt

Middle and top
$4^1/2$ cups (700 g) raw cashews, soaked overnight in cold water
1 cup (250 g) coconut cream
$1/2$ cup (175 g) honey
Grated zest and juice of 1 orange
1 tsp vanilla bean paste
1 drop orange essential oil (optional)
2 cups (250 g) raspberries, plus an extra handful
Dried rose petals, to garnish (optional)

Line a 20 cm (8 inch) square spring-form cake tin with baking paper. Mix all the base ingredients in a food processor until smooth; stop and scrape down the side every now and then. Press into the tin and pop in the freezer for 20 minutes.

For the middle and top layers, clean out the food processor, then tip in the drained cashews, coconut cream and honey. Blitz until smooth. Add the orange zest, orange juice, vanilla and orange oil, if using. Spoon half of the mixture over the base and return to the freezer for another 20 minutes.

Combine the raspberries and remaining cashew mixture and blitz until smooth. Spread over the middle layer. Top with the extra raspberries, then return to the freezer for at least 4 hours before cutting. Store in the freezer, allowing it to soften a little before serving with rose petals, if using.

MAKES 12–18 PIECES

You can use fresh or frozen raspberries for this slice.

Smoothies forever

Mango, chia, yoghurt and cardamom smoothie ~ Mint, cucumber, spinach and pineapple smoothie
Blueberry, walnut, banana and ginger smoothie ~ Coconut rough smoothie

I said this in the Spring chapter but I do like to push a point home! Smoothies are
excellent to make and give to anyone, especially new mums or friends with tender
tummies, low energy and/or zero time and energy to shop for and prepare healthy food.
A good smoothie repertoire is also handy for school holidays when the kids are too busy
racing to the beach, pool, bike track, wherever, to wait for a proper breakfast. I reason
that if they've put away one big smoothie, loaded with goodness and flavour, then they
have something healthy in their tummies and I haven't completely dropped the ball.

If you make up a few different smoothies, then even when there's nothing else
in the fridge you can still get some goodness into your day via a quick smoothie hit,
filling and full of condensed energy. When I was pregnant with our first child and
feeling nauseous ALL THE TIME, a cold mango smoothie at 4pm was a major
highlight of my day. My niece Grace named the Coconut rough smoothie and
she's spot on: the rich cacao and coconut flavours will appeal to any sweet tooth
and stop any chocolate cravings in their tracks.

SMOOTHIE NOTES

Dairy-based smoothies should be consumed the day they are made; non-dairy smoothies are fine for up to 2 days but will separate so need a good shake before drinking.

Always keep your smoothies cool. When transporting, please do so in a cool box or chiller bag with a few frozen bricks. And as usual when dropping off food that needs to be kept chilled, try to ensure that your lucky recipients are going to be home or home soon. If it's the latter, leave the box or bag beside the door or in a shady spot and come and pick it up again later.

Another option with these smoothies is to make up 'freezer bags' for you and your friends to tip into a blender with ice cubes and whizz up at will. Fruits such as bananas, mangoes, strawberries, raspberries and pineapple freeze well and make smoothies creamier and colder when whizzed up. Just keep things like soft herbs, greens and cucumbers separate as they don't love a freezer so much.

All four of these recipes make one or two serves. Simply combine all of the ingredients in a high-powered blender and whizz until smooth.

MANGO, CHIA, YOGHURT AND CARDAMOM SMOOTHIE

1 cup (185 g) chopped mango (about 1 mango)
1 Tbsp white chia seeds
1/4 cup (70 g) plain yoghurt
1 cup (250 ml) milk
A pinch of ground toasted cardamom (page 130)
4 ice cubes

MINT, CUCUMBER, SPINACH AND PINEAPPLE SMOOTHIE

1/2 cucumber, roughly chopped
1 handful baby English spinach
1 cup (160 g) roughly chopped pineapple
A few mint leaves
1 cup (250 ml) water or coconut water
Juice of 1/2 lime
4 ice cubes

BLUEBERRY, WALNUT, BANANA AND GINGER SMOOTHIE

1 cup (155 g) fresh or frozen blueberries
1 banana (preferably frozen)
10 walnuts
1 Tbsp coconut oil
3 cm (1 1/4 inch) piece ginger
1 cup (250 ml) water
4 ice cubes

COCONUT ROUGH SMOOTHIE

1 Tbsp raw cacao powder
1/4 cup (40 g) almonds
1/4 cup (20 g) shredded coconut
3 dates, pitted
1 Tbsp chia seeds
A pinch of sea salt
1 cup (250 ml) milk (dairy, nut or coconut)
4 ice cubes

This is a great way to quickly get some goodness into the day.

Catering for a crowd

Glazed ham ~ Jansson's temptation ~ Spiced cauliflower and chickpea salad
Will's crunchy wild rice and currant salad ~ Meringues ~ Poached apricots with ice cream

While this menu is, for my family at least, firmly anchored in Christmas, it would be just as welcome at any big gathering where bolstering food is called for: a 21st birthday, street party, wake, thank you party for staff, community group or local volunteer firefighters.

I know I'm not reinventing the wheel but sometimes it's nice to be reminded how good the simple classics are. They're classics for a reason, and if you feel you need to jazz things up a bit, get creative with the side salads. The two suggested here are my brothers' creations and are firm family favourites.

Big gatherings of any kind can bring their own spectrum of anxiety, so don't let food be one of them. Prepare this menu, delegate a few side dishes and then relax in the knowledge that your efforts will be universally appreciated.

GLAZED HAM

There are many good flavour combinations and options for glazing a ham; this one is my favourite. The inevitable leftovers will provide fillings for sandwiches, substance for frittatas and a tasty option to toss through pasta.

1 whole ham leg, around 6 kg (13½ lb)

Glaze
½ cup (125 ml) pomegranate molasses
Juice of 1 lime
Juice of 2 oranges
½ cup (175 g) honey
¼ cup (45 g) soft brown sugar

Combine all the glaze ingredients in a small saucepan. Cook over medium heat, stirring often, for 10 minutes or until you have a lovely glossy glaze.

Preheat the oven to 180°C (350°F). Use a sharp knife to cut around the ham shank, running the knife under the skin and right around the edge of the ham. Gently pull the skin back in one piece, using your fingers to push between the rind and fat. Reserve the skin for storing the ham. Score the fat in a diamond pattern. Cover the shank with foil.

Grab the biggest roasting tin you have and pour in water to come 1–2 cm (½–¾ inch) up the sides. Put a wire rack in the tin, pop the ham on top and brush with a third of the glaze. Place in the oven for 1 hour, pulling the ham out every 20 minutes to baste with the glaze and add more water if needed. Serve warm or at room temperature.

NOTE
Cooked ham must be stored in the fridge. Cover it with the skin you peeled off earlier, then place it in a fabric bag soaked in a vinegar solution (add a good splash of vinegar into a sink a third full of water, then dunk the bag in and give it a good hand wash). You can use a specific ham bag or a pillow case. Rinse and re-soak the ham bag in a vinegar solution every 3 days. Keep the ham for up to a week, but use your common sense – if it smells dodgy, it probably is.

SERVES 10–15

JANSSON'S TEMPTATION

I don't think we've ever had a Christmas when a potato bake of some kind wasn't on the table. If you don't think anchovies will fly at your place, then leave them out, but I find they 'melt' into the dish so beautifully, nobody notices them but they all appreciate the deep saltiness.

35 g (1¼ oz) butter, cut into cubes, plus extra
    for greasing
8 anchovy fillets (or to taste!), plus oil from the jar
1 brown onion, thinly sliced
200 ml (7 fl oz) single (pure) cream
½ cup (125 ml) milk
A good pinch of salt
A good pinch of freshly ground black pepper
1 kg (2 lb 4 oz) potatoes (Dutch cream are great
    for this), peeled and thinly sliced
1 cup (60 g) fresh breadcrumbs (ideally made from
    sourdough or a nice wholemeal or seeded bread)

Preheat the oven to 200°C (400°F). Brush a large ovenproof dish with butter.

Pour the oil from the anchovies into a frying pan over medium–low heat and add the onion and anchovies, breaking up the latter with a wooden spoon. Cook for about 5 minutes, stirring often.

Combine the cream, milk, salt and pepper in a saucepan and heat just to boiling point. Add the potato and simmer for about 15 minutes or until just tender when pierced with a sharp knife.

Carefully transfer half of the potato mixture to the ovenproof dish. Top with half of the onion mixture, then repeat with the remaining potato and onion mixtures. Sprinkle with the breadcrumbs and dot with the butter. Bake for 35 minutes or until the breadcrumbs are golden and crunchy. Serve warm or at room temperature.

SERVES 6–8

SPICED CAULIFLOWER AND CHICKPEA SALAD

This salad is great to take to a barbecue, picnic or other feast if you're asked to bring a plate – it's good served cold or at room temperature.

1 tsp ground coriander
1/2 tsp ground cumin
1/2 tsp ground turmeric
1/2 tsp chilli flakes (to taste)
1 tsp caster sugar
1/2 tsp sea salt
1 cauliflower, cut into florets
1/3 cup (80 ml) olive oil
2 brown onions, thinly sliced
3/4 cup (150 g) dried chickpeas, soaked overnight in cold water, then cooked until tender, or 400 g (14 oz) tin chickpeas, rinsed and drained
1 handful coriander (cilantro) leaves
1 handful flat-leaf parsley leaves
2 handfuls mixed salad leaves
Juice of 1 lemon

Preheat the oven to 200°C (400°F). Combine all of the spices, sugar and salt in a small bowl. Place the cauliflower on a baking tray. Drizzle with a little of the olive oil, sprinkle with the spice mix and rub to combine. Roast the cauliflower for 35 minutes or until it's beginning to char on the edges.

Meanwhile, heat the remaining olive oil in a frying pan over medium–low heat and cook the onion for 15 minutes or until caramelised.

In a large serving bowl, toss together the cauliflower, chickpeas and onion. Just before serving, add the herbs and salad leaves, drizzle with the lemon juice and season to taste.

SERVES 6 (AS A SIDE SALAD)

WILL'S CRUNCHY WILD RICE AND CURRANT SALAD

Another good option to prepare ahead and transport, this salad is also substantial enough to serve on its own.

1/3 cup (65 g) wild rice
1 1/2 cups (300 g) basmati rice
1/3 cup (80 ml) olive oil
2 red onions, finely diced
1/2 cup (75 g) sunflower seeds
1/2 cup (75 g) pepitas (pumpkin seeds)
1/4 cup (40 g) sesame seeds
1 tsp cumin seeds
1 cup (140 g) dried or fresh currants
1 handful mint leaves
1 handful flat-leaf parsley
2 handfuls baby English spinach

Dressing
1/4 cup (60 ml) olive oil
2 tsp dijon mustard
2 Tbsp red wine vinegar

Put the wild rice in a small saucepan and cover with cold water. Bring to the boil, then reduce the heat and simmer for about 35 minutes or until tender (you may need to top up the water during this time). Rinse and drain, then set aside.

Meanwhile, cook the basmati rice according to the packet instructions (I use the absorption method).

Heat 2 tablespoons of the olive oil in a frying pan over medium–low heat. Cook the onion for 15 minutes or until caramelised. Transfer to a plate.

Wipe the frying pan clean and then return to the heat. Cook the sunflower seeds, pepitas, sesame seeds and cumin seeds until toasted and just beginning to pop.

Combine the rices in a large bowl. Add the onion, toasted seeds, currants, mint, parsley and spinach.

Shake the dressing ingredients in a jar until combined. Pour over the salad and toss, then season to taste.

SERVES 6 (AS A SIDE SALAD)

MERINGUES

My paternal grandmother, Mary, made the world's best meringues – hard on the outside and chewy inside. After Sunday lunch she'd put a big plate of them on the table with a bowl of whipped cream and a bowl of passionfruit pulp. We'd sandwich two meringues together with that tangy cream mixture and they were everything. Here they are with poached apricots and ice cream.

Meringues can be a bit tricky to master, I know. The main thing really is getting the measure of your oven and not burning them or turning them brown. My advice is to always err on the side of a lower oven temperature and longer cooking time, rather than rushing and burning them.

3 egg whites
A pinch of salt
¾ cup (165 g) caster sugar

Preheat the oven to 130°C (250°F). Line two large baking trays with baking paper.

Place the egg whites and salt in the bowl of an electric mixer. Whisk until soft peaks form, then begin adding the sugar, 1 tablespoon at a time. Keep mixing for 6 minutes or until glossy and stiff.

Using two tablespoons, make mounds of the meringue mixture on the baking trays, leaving about 5 cm (2 inches) between them. Bake for 45 minutes, then turn off the oven and leave inside to cool.

VARIATIONS
Crush the meringues and serve with whipped cream, a fresh apricot purée and berries (Eton mess at its best).

Make the meringues as discs, top with a little whipped cream and perch half a poached peach, pear or quince on top. Sprinkle with praline and maybe a cloud of Persian fairy floss.

Serve as a pavlova, topped with whipped cream, passionfruit and berries.

MAKES 15–20

My grandmother made the world's best meringues – crunchy on the outside and chewy inside.

POACHED APRICOTS WITH ICE CREAM

Cut 1 kg (2 lb 4 oz) apricots in half, discarding the stones. Combine ¹/2 cup (110 g) caster sugar, ¹/2 cup (125 ml) wine and 1 tsp vanilla bean paste in a large saucepan and bring to the boil. Add the apricots, then reduce the heat to a low simmer and cover the mixture with a piece of baking paper. Cook for 5 minutes or until the apricots are soft, then remove from the heat. Store in the fridge.

To make the ice cream, churn 1 quantity custard (page 154) in an ice cream machine. Alternatively, freeze the mixture for 1 hour, then whisk until smooth. Repeat the freezing and whisking three times; this breaks up the ice crystals so you have a lovely smooth ice cream. Serves 4–6

Always waiting for special occasions to do special things lets too many days pass by without particular note.

Morning tea in the orchard

Fig and peach custard tarts ~ Vanilla, peach and mint iced tea

'How we spend our days is, of course, how we spend our lives.' I love this line
from Annie Dillard's book, *The Writing Life*. And it reminds me that always waiting for
special occasions to do special things lets too many days pass without particular note.

A morning tea for your co-workers, a welcome to the area present for new neighbours,
a birthday morning tea for a friend and so on; these occasions can be elevated to
memorable moments thanks to someone going to the moderate effort of buying or
making a nice cake or tart, producing a tablecloth and mixing a jug of iced mint tea.

Cue this late summer spread, orchard optional – all you need is a nature strip, a kitchen
bench, an office board room, wherever... venue isn't key, but the sentiment is.

FIG AND PEACH CUSTARD TARTS

This blueprint custard tart recipe is an absolute winner, and to make it even easier, you could just buy a ready-rolled sheet of shortcrust pastry or even a frozen tart shell. Then whisk together the custard filling, top with fruit and it's ready to go.

The tart is good either warm or at room temperature. Store it in the fridge for up to 2 days, then gently reheat before serving.

Sweet shortcrust pastry
1⅓ cups (200 g) plain flour, plus
    extra for dusting
A pinch of salt
⅓ cup (40 g) icing sugar
150 g (5½ oz) chilled unsalted butter,
    cut into small cubes
¼ cup (60 ml) chilled water

Custard filling
1 cup (250 ml) single (pure) cream
2 eggs
¼ cup (55 g) caster sugar
1 vanilla bean
4 figs, peaches or nectarines, or
    1 cup (150 g) berries or poached
    fruit (quinces would be beautiful)

To make the pastry, combine the flour, salt and icing sugar on a work surface. Bring into a small mound and make a well in the centre. Fill the well with the cubed butter and a splash of the chilled water. Use the heels of your hands to bring everything together, working the butter into the flour and adding more water as needed. Keep working and smooshing with the heels of your hands until you have a rough dough. Shape into a disc, cover and place in the fridge to rest for 30 minutes.

Lightly dust your work surface with flour, then gently roll out the pastry into a large round, about 3 mm (⅛ inch) thick. Gently drape it over the rolling pin and unroll it into a loose-based fluted tart tin, about 23 cm (9 inches) wide and 3 cm (1¼ inches) deep. Press the pastry down into the crease where the base meets the side. Roll the rolling pin over the top of the tin, cutting away the excess pastry to create a nice neat edge. Return to the fridge for 30 minutes before blind baking.

Preheat the oven to 200°C (400°F). Prick the base of the pastry a few times with a fork. Line with baking paper and fill with pastry weights, uncooked rice or dried beans. Blind bake for 10 minutes, then remove the weights and baking paper and bake for a further 10 minutes or until the pastry looks pale and dry.

Meanwhile, make the custard filling. Combine the cream, eggs and sugar in a bowl. Using a small sharp knife, cut the vanilla bean in half lengthways, scrape out the seeds, add them to the cream mixture and whisk together. Set aside while you slice the fruit.

Pour the custard into the tart shell and top with the fruit. Bake for 20–25 minutes or until the custard is just turning golden.

MAKES ONE 23 CM (9 INCH) TART

VANILLA, PEACH AND MINT ICED TEA

A jug of this refreshing iced tea goes beautifully with either of the custard tarts on page 100 and it makes a welcome change from the usual hot morning cuppa. It's also a lovely treat to make up and give someone, and will keep in the fridge for a couple of days. Serve it over plenty of ice.

$^1/_3$ cup (30 g) green tea leaves or 6 green tea bags
1 Tbsp roughly chopped fresh ginger
6 cups (1.5 litres) boiling water
2 peaches or nectarines, sliced
1 handful mint leaves
Ice, to serve

Vanilla syrup
1 cup (220 g) sugar
1 vanilla bean, split lengthways

To make the vanilla syrup, put the sugar in a small saucepan with 2 cups (500 ml) water. Scrape the vanilla seeds into the pan and add the vanilla bean. Heat until the sugar dissolves.

Combine the tea, ginger and boiling water in a large heatproof jug and leave to brew for 5 minutes. Discard the tea leaves or bags, pour in 2 cups (500 ml) of the vanilla syrup and the vanilla bean, then transfer to the fridge to cool.

When ready to serve, check the flavour – is it too strong, too sweet or not sweet enough? Add more water or vanilla syrup to taste. Transfer to a large serving jug and add the sliced fruit, mint leaves and ice.

MAKES ABOUT 8 CUPS (2 LITRES)

I like to have a jug of this ready and waiting in the fridge during summer.

Christmas baking

Brunekager ~ Christmas trail mix ~ Mini spiced Christmas wreaths

Summer in Australia means Christmas, and the perfect opportunity to fill the kitchen with kids, get the Christmas tunes cranking and bake up a batch of festive cheer. This baking party is a craft and cooking activity rolled into one. Everyone can help, whether it's cutting out biscuits, measuring and packaging trail mix or braiding dough wreaths. You might even get some offers to help with the washing up and taste the Christmas goodies.

BRUNEKAGER

My family's version of these gently spiced Danish 'brown biscuits' are my favourite. They're wonderful for cutting into shapes or making into classic thin rounds. They last for ages and make the kitchen smell nice and homely. You'll also find these crumbled into Cold vanilla and buttermilk soup (page 133) and tucked into a basket of spring goodies (page 15).

2 cups (300 g) plain flour, plus extra for dusting
$^{1}/_{2}$ tsp bicarbonate of soda
2 tsp ground ginger
1 tsp ground cinnamon
$^{1}/_{2}$ tsp ground toasted cardamom (page 130)
A good grinding of black pepper
A pinch of salt
$^{3}/_{4}$ cup (165 g) firmly packed soft brown sugar
125 g (4$^{1}/_{2}$ oz) chilled butter, cut into cubes
$^{1}/_{4}$ cup (90 g) honey
2 Tbsp boiling water

Preheat the oven to 180°C (350°F). Line two large baking trays with baking paper.

Combine the flour, bicarbonate of soda, spices, salt, brown sugar and butter in the bowl of your food processor and blitz until the mixture resembles fine breadcrumbs.

Whisk the honey and boiling water in a small jug. Pour into the food processor and blitz again for a few seconds. Turn the mixture out onto a work surface and bring together into a disc. Wrap in plastic wrap and place in the fridge to chill for 30 minutes.

Turn the dough out onto a lightly floured surface and divide it into three pieces. Roll out each piece of dough to about 3 mm ($^{1}/_{8}$ inch) thick. This is the fun part – get out your cookie cutters and cut shapes from the dough. Transfer to the trays and bake for 10–12 minutes or until golden. Let the biscuits cool on wire racks, then ice or decorate them as you like.

VARIATION
These are great in ice cream sandwiches. Cut the biscuits into rounds using an 8–10 cm (3$^{1}/_{4}$–4 inch) cookie cutter or glass. Buy or make a nice vanilla ice cream, allow it to soften a little and then spread it out on a shallow baking tray. Return the ice cream to the freezer to firm up a little, then cut it into circles using the same cutter as before. Return to the freezer again to firm up, then sandwich each ice cream round between two biscuits. Keep in the freezer until ready to serve.

MAKES ABOUT 30

CHRISTMAS TRAIL MIX

Trail mix is great for car trips, work snacks and, of course, as sustenance when out trail walking. Although I've called this one Christmas trail mix, it's excellent at any time of year. Combine 1 cup (160 g) oven-roasted almonds, 1 cup (45 g) pretzels, $^{1}/_{2}$ cup (75 g) pepitas (pumpkin seeds), $^{1}/_{2}$ cup (110 g) crystallised ginger, $^{1}/_{2}$ cup (75 g) dried cranberries and 1 cup (140 g) roughly chopped white chocolate.

MINI SPICED CHRISTMAS WREATHS

1 quantity basic sweet dough (page 249)
Icing sugar, for dusting

Filling
100 g (3½ oz) butter, softened
½ cup (110 g) firmly packed soft brown sugar
1 tsp ground cinnamon
¼ tsp freshly grated nutmeg

Preheat the oven to 180°C (350°F). Line two large baking trays with baking paper.

To make the filling, mix the soft butter, sugar and spices together.

Turn the dough out onto a lightly floured work surface and gently cut it into six even pieces. Roll out one piece of dough until you have a rectangle about 30 x 20 cm (12 x 8 inches). Spread the dough with one-sixth of the filling. Gently, but as tightly as you can, roll the dough from the longest edge into a long sausage. Use a serrated knife to slice the dough in half lengthways to make two long half-cylinders. Put the halves next to each other, cut sides up, and braid together, forming a wreath as you go. It sounds a bit tricky but really it's not – just press the ends together and place one piece of dough over the other, always with the cut side facing up, then lay the other piece over the top and so on, working it into a circular wreath shape. Press the ends together.

Repeat with the remaining dough and filling, then gently transfer the wreaths to the trays. Bake for about 25 minutes or until the wreaths are risen and golden. Dust with icing sugar and serve warm. If you're serving these the next day, warm them up in the oven.

MAKES 6

Working with buttery, yeasted, sweet dough is my happy place. I often make different versions of this recipe, from the individual wreaths here to a large one filled with blood orange curd (page 250). Don't be put off by the yeast or by the technique – both are easy to handle and the result is far more impressive than it is difficult. The braiding might take a little bit of practice, but don't worry if it isn't perfect, it will still be delicious!

Summer care package

Honey-soy chicken legs ~ Spinach and ham tart ~ Brown sugar and spice zucchini loaf

As I write this, in February 2018, a bushfire is burning a few kilometres from our farm. My husband, Tim, is out there with our local Rural Fire Services brigade, along with over a hundred more volunteers on the ground. In the sky is the enormous Nancy Bird, a VLAT (acronym for the somewhat unimaginative name of this fire retardant dropping/life saving Very Large Air Tanker), plus a Hercules plane and a number of helicopters dropping water and working hard to hold containment lines. It's a scary roller-coaster for the rest of us; one minute I look out of the window and think it's all going to be fine, the next it feels as if the billowing smoke is within arm's reach. So with sprinklers on the roof, water pumps and generators at the ready, I sit and wait. While, in the kitchen, batches of biscuits, curry and quiche are working their way through the oven, ready to be dropped off at the control centre to help sustain the wonderful people protecting our houses and livelihoods.

At times like this, people want simple food. Food that their kids will eat too, that can be eaten as it is or needs just a quick burst in the microwave or on the stovetop. Because when people are stressed, hungry, tired and sick of toasted sandwiches, a delivery of simple, ready-to-eat, comforting family food can be a godsend.

HONEY-SOY CHICKEN LEGS

I know I'm re-inventing the wheel here, but these are always such a hit with adults and kids alike that I thought it was worth including them. Mum often made these and I thought they were the most exotic, delicious meal ever. I make them for my kids to the same enthusiastic reception.

8 chicken legs
½ cup (125 ml) soy sauce
⅔ cup (235 g) honey
2 garlic cloves, finely chopped
6 cm (2½ inch) piece ginger, finely chopped
Sesame seeds, for sprinkling

Put the chicken legs in a large non-reactive bowl. Whisk together the soy sauce, honey, garlic and ginger. Pour the marinade over the chicken legs and toss well. Cover and place in the fridge for a few hours or overnight.

Preheat the oven to 200°C (400°F). Remove the chicken legs from the marinade and place on a foil-lined baking tray. Sprinkle with sesame seeds and bake for 35 minutes or until the chicken is cooked through – pierce the fleshy part of one leg and check carefully for 'done-ness'. Serve either hot or from the fridge (they're really good cold).

MAKES 8

SPINACH AND HAM TART

This tart transports well and is lovely at room temperature or straight from the oven. It's also a great way to use up left-over Christmas ham.

1 quantity rough puff pastry (page 40)
2 eggs
½ cup (125 ml) single (pure) cream
½ cup (50 g) finely grated parmesan cheese
Grated zest of 1 lemon
1 cup (150 g) roughly chopped, thick-sliced ham
½ cup (100 g) blanched, finely chopped
    English spinach

Roll out the pastry on a lightly floured surface until about 5 mm (¼ inch) thick. Drape the pastry over the rolling pin and unroll it into a loose-based fluted tart tin – mine is 20 cm (8 inches) wide and 3 cm (1¼ inches) deep. The pastry will shrink back into the tin when cooking, so minimise this by leaving extra at the top and really pushing the pastry down and into each indent in the side of the tin. Trim the edge, leaving about 5 mm (¼ inch) extra. Return to the fridge for 30 minutes.

Preheat the oven to 200°C (400°F). Prick the pastry base with the tines of a fork. Line with baking paper and fill the base with pastry weights, uncooked rice or dried beans (this stops the base rising during baking). Bake for 10 minutes, then gently remove the weights and baking paper and cook for another 5–10 minutes or until the pastry is just lightly golden and looks dry. Meanwhile, prepare the tart filling.

Whisk together the eggs and cream. Season to taste, then add half of the parmesan and the lemon zest. Pour into the pastry and add the ham and chopped spinach. Sprinkle with the remaining parmesan and some black pepper. Bake for 25–30 minutes or until the top is golden and just firm to touch.

SERVES 6–8

BROWN SUGAR AND SPICE ZUCCHINI LOAF

A good zucchini loaf recipe is handy in late summer when every gardener seems to be swimming in zucchini and bringing bags of them to work in an effort to offload their bounty. Here's my favourite way to make good use of this generous vegetable. Slice and package the loaf to serve fresh, or toast it and top it with a dollop of my Home-made crème fraîche (page 130).

500 g (1 lb 2 oz) zucchini (courgettes), grated (about 3 large zucchini)
¼ cup (55 g) caster sugar
1⅔ cups (250 g) wholemeal plain flour
2 tsp baking powder
2 tsp ground ginger
½ tsp ground nutmeg
½ tsp ground cinnamon
A pinch of freshly ground black pepper
A pinch of salt
1 cup (220 g) firmly packed soft brown sugar
3 large eggs
1 cup (250 ml) extra virgin olive oil
1 tsp vanilla bean paste

Preheat the oven to 180°C (350°F). Grease and line one large loaf tin – mine is rather long, about 28 x 13 cm (11¼ x 5 inches) – or two smaller ones with baking paper.

In a small bowl, mix the zucchini with half of the caster sugar. Place the mixture in a colander over the same bowl and weigh it down with a plate and a tin of tomatoes or similar and leave for at least 10 minutes so as much liquid drains away as possible.

Whisk the flour, baking powder, spices and salt in a large bowl. In a separate bowl, combine the remaining caster sugar with the brown sugar, eggs, olive oil and vanilla, whisking until all the ingredients are really well combined. Gently fold the wet and dry ingredients together. Squeeze any excess liquid out of the zucchini, then fold the zucchini into the batter.

Pour the batter into the tin, smooth the top and bake for 1 hour or until the loaf is beginning to pull away from the sides of the tin and a skewer inserted into the centre comes out clean. Leave in the tin for 5 minutes before turning it out onto a wire rack to cool.

SERVES 8

Summer fruit harvest

Cherry and rose petal jam ~ Apricot and vanilla jam ~ Bottled fruit ~ Fruit cobbler
Stone fruit and redcurrant chutney ~ Raspberry vinegar cordial

When I moved to northern Italy in my late twenties, the first couple of months were dreadfully lonely. I didn't know a soul and I didn't speak Italian – two major road blocks when it came to making friends. I'd catch the train to Turin every Saturday and wander around the outdoor food market. There I dreamt of buying the enormous bunches of mint, asparagus, artichokes and tomatoes to prepare feasts for my friends, before remembering I didn't have any (cue violins). Instead I'd buy bags of strawberries, and spend Sunday making jam. The familiar ritual and smells made my dark apartment feel homely for a few hours at least.

My Italian slowly improved, and I kept taking my work colleagues jars of jam. Gradually they began to involve me in their family outings, drinks, dinners and Sunday picnics. Soon I had a life that was exciting and romantic enough to keep me there – for three years. It turned out to be a wonderful experience, but even now the smell of strawberry jam pulls the shutters of loneliness down fast.

All of this is to say that I will never write a strawberry jam recipe. EVER. I will, instead, offer you these gems: cherry and rose petal, and apricot and vanilla. And because there's nothing as satisfying as putting away a glut of seasonal produce for the lean winter and early spring months, I've included my method for bottling fruit and a few other favourite fruit recipes.

There are few things as satisfying
as putting away a glut of
seasonal produce.

NOTES ON JAM MAKING

~ The faster jam is made, the fresher and fruitier it tastes, which is why it's best to make small batches of jam – it's easier to cook faster in small quantities.

~ Slightly underripe fruit is best to use in jam, because it will have more acidity.

~ Use a pan with a wide base so that the fruit cooks more evenly and, again, faster.

~ Sterilise the jars before you start – I wash mine well in a hot dishwasher, then heat them in a 180°C (350°F) oven for 15 minutes.

~ You can tie up the lemon pips in a piece of muslin if you want to remove them before bottling. Don't leave them out entirely, as they add lots of good natural pectin that helps the jam set.

~ When jars and bottles are sterilised properly, the preserves reach setting point before bottling, and they are stored in a cool, dark place, jams should have a shelf life of at least 9–12 months, and cordials of 6 weeks. If you're in any doubt at all, store them in the fridge.

CHERRY AND ROSE PETAL JAM

1 kg (2 lb 4 oz) sugar
1 tsp pectin (see Note)
1 kg (2 lb 4 oz) ripe cherries
2 lemons
2 handfuls unsprayed rose petals

Put a couple of small plates in the freezer. Pour the sugar into a large bowl and add the pectin, whisking so it's well distributed.

Now get started on pitting the cherries. (I splurged a few years ago and bought a $20 cherry pitter. It comes into its own every December and I highly recommend any cherry lovers buy one – you'll thank me!)

Place the pitted cherries in a large saucepan and pour in the sugar. Cut the lemons in half and squeeze in the juice and pips, then gently stir to combine. If you have a sugar thermometer, attach it to the side of the pan.

Bring the mixture to a slow simmer. Once the sugar has melted, bring to a rolling boil. Cook, stirring every now and then so the jam doesn't catch or burn on the bottom, for 10 minutes or until the temperature reaches jam setting point – 105°C (221°F). If you don't have a sugar thermometer, do the 'plate test': after about 10 minutes, drop a teaspoon of the jam onto one of the plates you put in the freezer, wait for about 10 seconds, then push your finger through the middle of the jam. If it wrinkles and resists a little then it has reached setting point. If the jam is still runny, cook it for another 5–10 minutes before testing again.

Remove from the heat and stir in the rose petals. Ladle the jam into sterilised jars, filling each right to the top. Screw on the lids tightly and invert the jars onto a board covered with a tea towel (inverting the jars helps create a seal).

NOTE
Adding pectin is optional, but with low-pectin fruits like cherries (and strawberries, blueberries, peaches, pears, figs, etc.), I usually just throw in a little extra so I don't end up with a syrup rather than a jam. You can find pectin in most supermarkets or online via preserving websites.

MAKES ABOUT 3 JARS

I once spent a few freezing days in Venice right before Christmas. One of my main motivations for the trip was to visit the Monastero di San Lazzaro degli Armeni, an Armenian monastery that sits on a tiny island. Its scholarly monks are known for the rose petal jam they make on the island, and the idea of this confection and its creators had captivated me. I'll never forget sitting in the chapel on that bone-chillingly cold day, the pews giving off a hint of the rose oil that's regularly rubbed into them, and feeling overwhelmed by the place and the disappointing fact that they were out of jam.

This is my ode to that moment. I made my rose petal jam on a bright, sunny day in my neighbour's kitchen 16 years later, with her happy babies playing at our feet, the cricket on the radio and my own family just down the road.

This lovely jam is a firm favourite of mine. It makes enough to fill about 8 medium-sized jam jars, but this depends, of course, on the size of the jars you use.

APRICOT AND VANILLA JAM

3.5 kg (7 lb 14 oz) apricots
2 vanilla beans, split lengthways
1 lemon
2.5 kg (5 lb 8 oz) sugar

Place a couple of small plates in the freezer. Preheat the oven to 160°C (320°F).

Cut the apricots in half, removing and reserving the stones. Cut each apricot half into quarters and place in a large heavy-based saucepan or stockpot.

Crack 15 of the apricot stones to reveal the almond-shaped kernel inside. Place these in a shallow dish and cover with boiling water for 5 minutes, then drain and roughly chop (make sure there aren't any hard pieces of shell in there). Add to the saucepan with the apricots.

Scrape the vanilla seeds into the saucepan and add the vanilla beans. Pour in ½ cup (125 ml) water. Cut the lemon in half and squeeze in the juice and pips, then add the lemon halves.

Bring to the boil, stirring often so that nothing sticks to the bottom of the pan and burns. Boil for 10 minutes, at which point the apricots will be lovely and soft. Meanwhile, tip the sugar into a large stainless-steel bowl or baking tray and place it in the oven to warm up – about 6 minutes will do the trick.

After the fruit has been cooking for 10 minutes, pour in the hot sugar. If you have a sugar thermometer, attach it to the side of the pan and cook the jam over high heat, stirring often, for 15 minutes or until the temperature reaches jam setting point – 105°C (221°F). If you don't have a thermometer, do the 'plate test': after 15 minutes, dollop a teaspoon of the jam onto one of the plates you put in the freezer, wait for about 10 seconds, then push your finger through the middle of the jam. If the jam wrinkles and resists a little then it has reached setting point. If it is still runny, cook it for another 5–10 minutes before testing again. Discard the lemon halves.

Ladle the jam into sterilised jars, filling each right to the top. Screw on the lids tightly and invert the jars onto a board covered with a tea towel (inverting the jars helps create a seal).

NOTE
The faster the jam is made, the better it tastes, which is why you warm the sugar before adding it to the fruit. If you added all that cold sugar it would slow down the cooking process.

MAKES ABOUT 8 JARS

I can't imagine a more delicious combination of apricots and vanilla.

BOTTLED FRUIT

Also known as heat preserving, bottling is a fantastic way to preserve seasonal produce. It means that in deepest winter, when the fruit bowl is empty, you can reach into the pantry for a jar of bright and sunny preserved apricots to spoon over your porridge. And in other good news, the whole process – while it can be a touch hot, sticky and time consuming – is as easy as the pie you can make later with your bottled fruit! I don't recommend bottling fruit when you are rushed in any way, so invite some friends over and make an afternoon of it. Set up afternoon tea, play some great tunes and have a good chat while you chop, wash and pack fruit into jars.

FRUIT TO PRESERVE

~ **Apricots** with toasted cardamom pods

~ **Peaches** with ginger syrup (when making the sugar syrup, add 1 teaspoon grated ginger)

~ **Figs** with vanilla syrup (see page 105)

~ **Plums** with spiced syrup (when making the sugar syrup, add a cinnamon stick, star anise and some ground nutmeg)

THE BASIC BOTTLING RECIPE

Make up a light sugar syrup (1 part sugar to 4 parts water). You can use a heavier syrup if you like: that's the joy of preserving – you control the sugar and flavours, so own it, ladies and gents! Combine the sugar with the water in a saucepan and heat it, stirring, until the sugar dissolves.

Sterilise your jars and lids before you begin by running them through the hottest cycle on the dishwasher or washing thoroughly, then drying them in a 180°C (350°F) oven for 15 minutes.

Next prepare your fruit. If I'm using stone fruit, I cut it in half, discard the stones and sometimes cut it into quarters – it's all very basic but the fruit needs to be in even-sized pieces. Pack the fruit as tightly as possible into your sterilised jars (use a wooden spoon to push the pieces down, but don't be rough and bruise the fruit). Pour in the sugar syrup, leaving about 1 cm (½ inch) of space at the top.

Slide a knife down and around the inside of each jar to release any air bubbles, then give the jar a good tap on the bench. Seal, then place in the preserving unit and follow the instructions. If you're using a stockpot or saucepan, pour in enough cold water to come at least three-quarters of the way up the sides of your jars, bring to the boil, then turn down and simmer on the lowest heat for 2 hours.

Remove the jars from the water using either tongs or a tea towel with great care and let them cool, then store in a dark corner of the kitchen.

STOCKPOT OR PRESERVING UNIT?

I have a great old Fowlers preserving unit that makes the whole process easy. You can source new and used kits online or from speciality shops. You'll also need to invest in Fowlers jars, lids, clips and rings. If you do go down this route, may I suggest joining the Facebook group 'Fowlers Vacola Users'? Once inside this treasure trove of knowledge, you can ask any preserving question and be the recipient of much generous and accurate advice. While a Fowlers unit does make bottling easier, a big stockpot or pan and clean glass jars and metal lids will also do the job. If going down this road, it's important to stop the jars from touching the bottom of the pan – place them on a small metal rack or a folded tea towel and then wrap each jar in a tea towel so they don't clang against each other and break.

FRUIT COBBLER

Delicious, simple and comforting – this cherry cobbler is my kind of baking. Basically a sponge topped with fruit, then baked and sprinkled with sugar, it's the sort of thing your gran might have served with Sunday lunch. It tastes honest and good, like proper puddings should. And it's a fabulous way to showcase your preserved fruit through the bare winter months. That said, it's also lovely made with fresh seasonal fruit at any time of the year. Thank you to Lesley Russell for sharing this recipe with me.

120 g (4¼ oz) butter, softened,
  plus extra for greasing
½ cup (110 g) caster sugar, plus
  extra for sprinkling
2 eggs
1⅔ cups (250 g) self-raising flour
⅓ cup (80 ml) milk
2 cups (400 g) preserved cherries,
  apricots, plums or peaches

Preheat the oven to 180°C (350°F). Butter a shallow ovenproof dish.

Cream the butter and sugar together until light and fluffy. Add the eggs one at a time, beating well after each addition. Stir in the flour and milk to make a fairly stiff batter.

Spread the batter over the base of the dish. Arrange the fruit over the batter, leaving gaps here and there. Don't worry if a bit of juice comes with the fruit – it makes the cobbler more moist.

Bake in the centre of the oven for 30 minutes or until cooked through when tested with a skewer. As soon as you take the cobbler out of the oven, sprinkle it with extra sugar. Serve immediately, with cream or ice cream.

SERVES 6–8

OTHER THINGS TO MAKE WITH BOTTLED FRUIT

~ Blitz 1 cup (200 g) preserved apricots with ½ cup (125 ml) of the preserving liquid in a blender. Stir the purée through whipped cream and serve with crushed meringues (page 98) and amaretti biscuits for a fancy Eton mess.

~ Pour a jar of preserved stone fruit or figs into an ovenproof dish, cover with the crumble mixture from page 155 and bake until golden and bubbling. Serve with ice cream and custard (page 154).

~ Gently warm bottled fruit to serve with porridge, cream and a sprinkle of Sweet dukkah (page 134) for a special winter breakfast.

~ Serve with plain yoghurt and a little Granola (page 33).

~ Fold through a simple butter cake batter.

~ Add to smoothies.

~ Serve piled onto Fluffy pancakes (page 224) with plain yoghurt.

STONE FRUIT AND REDCURRANT CHUTNEY

This is absolutely delicious with warm ham and crusty bread, dolloped on a quiche or frittata, served with Pork and pistachio terrine (page 87), spread over a chunk of good cheddar cheese or spooned onto plates of barbecued short-loin lamb chops or sausages. In short: it's very useful and makes a great present.

If you're new to the world of preserving, this is a good place to start. Chutneys are much more forgiving than jam, there are far less rules and there's more room to improvise with ingredients. I've used apricots, but you can use any stone fruit: peaches, nectarines or plums would all be great. The redcurrants add a gorgeous pop of flavour and colour, but if they aren't available, just make up the weight with more stone fruit.

1 kg (2 lb 4 oz) stone fruit
2 brown onions, finely diced
1²/₃ cups (250 g) dried cranberries
1²/₃ cups (250 g) fresh or frozen redcurrants
2 cups (440 g) firmly packed soft brown sugar
6 cm (2¹/₂ inch) piece ginger, peeled and
* finely chopped*
1 Tbsp sea salt
1 cinnamon stick
A good pinch of chilli flakes, or to taste
2 cups (500 ml) apple cider vinegar

Halve the stone fruit, discarding the stones, and cut into quarters.

Combine the fruit and all the remaining ingredients in a large heavy-based saucepan over medium–low heat. Cook for a few minutes until the sugar dissolves, then increase the heat to high and bring to the boil. Reduce the heat to medium–low and cook for about 45 minutes or until the chutney is glossy and thick. Transfer to sterilised jars to store.

MAKES ABOUT 3 JARS

RASPBERRY VINEGAR CORDIAL

This recipe comes via my husband's late father, Andrew. Andrew was a much-loved country vet and deer farmer (he began our journey with Mandagery Creek Venison some 30 years ago). He introduced me to this recipe, with memories of his grandmother making it for him as a boy. If you're lucky enough to have raspberries growing at home, do try this lovely and different way of preserving them.

I'd never tried raspberry vinegar cordial before Andrew suggested it and I was really pleasantly surprised. It's sweet and fruity, but balanced with the vinegar's acidity. It's very refreshing served over crushed ice with mineral water. You could throw in a splash of vodka if you're feeling festive.

500 g (1 lb 2 oz) raspberries
2 cups (500 ml) white wine vinegar
4 cups (880 g) sugar

Wash the raspberries, then drain and place in a large bowl. Add the vinegar and use a wooden spoon, pestle or the end of a rolling pin to bash the raspberries into the vinegar until you have a rough slush. Cover with a tea towel and set aside for a day for the raspberries and vinegar to get to know each other (don't put it in the fridge).

Strain the raspberry mixture through a fine sieve or muslin bag, extracting as much liquid as possible. The more force you use, the cloudier it will become – that doesn't bother me but if you want a clearer cordial, don't force the mixture through the sieve.

Transfer the raspberry liquid to a saucepan and bring to the boil, then add the sugar and whisk to combine. Boil for 5 minutes, then pour into sterilised bottles and immediately seal.

MAKES ABOUT 2 CUPS (500 ML)

If you're new to preserving, it's a good
idea to start with a chutney.

A tray of seasonal fruit always
  makes a beautiful summertime gift.

Gift trays and baskets

Rosemary crackers and honey labna ~ Home-made crème fraîche and toasted cardamom sugar
Vanilla salt ~ Lime chilli salt ~ Cold vanilla and buttermilk soup ~ Chocolate sauce and sweet dukkah

One of my mum's dear friends, who recently finished breast cancer treatment, told me she'd been blown away by the thoughtful care packages from friends and family. The most wonderful discovery was a tray of fresh figs and a hunk of blue cheese on her doorstep after coming home from chemo one summer afternoon. Another memorable gift was a basket containing soft socks, magazines and boiled sweets, and the loan of a beloved cashmere wrap. Small slices of comfort in and amongst all the discomfort of that horrible illness.

Who wouldn't love a tray of fresh, seasonal fruit, accompanied by any of the following delightful combinations? Minimal cooking, lots of flavour and such a good simple present for anyone. Including yourself.

Rosemary crackers and honey labna with figs

Packaged up in a little pot with some crackers and fresh figs, honey labna is such a treat.

ROSEMARY CRACKERS
AND HONEY LABNA (WITH FIGS)

Rosemary crackers are beautiful with fresh figs and my honey labna, but also with dips or any soft white cheese. If you have a pasta machine then pull it out for this recipe – you can use a rolling pin but the crackers won't be quite as thin. Honey labna is best friends with all summer fruits.

Rosemary crackers
1 cup (150 g) plain flour, plus extra
   for dusting
A pinch of sugar
2 Tbsp rosemary, finely chopped
⅓ cup (80 ml) olive oil
2 Tbsp honey
Sea salt, for sprinkling

Honey labna
500 g (1 lb 2 oz) Greek-style yoghurt
2 Tbsp honey
1 tsp salt
1 vanilla bean, split lengthways

Rosemary crackers
Combine the flour, sugar, rosemary, olive oil and ¼ cup (60 ml) water in a large bowl and mix well. Turn out onto a work surface and knead until you have a smooth dough, about 2–3 minutes. Cover with plastic wrap and leave to rest in the fridge for 30 minutes.

Preheat the oven to 180°C (350°F). Line three large baking trays with baking paper.

Divide the dough into three pieces. Take one piece of dough, leaving the rest covered with the plastic wrap so it doesn't dry out. Flatten the dough between your hands so you have a rough rectangle. Lightly dust it with flour, then feed it through the widest setting of a pasta machine. Repeat with the next setting, and again until you end up with a lovely long, thin sheet of dough. Cut the sheet in half and place it on one of the trays. Repeat with the remaining dough.

Combine the honey and 2 teaspoons water in a small saucepan and stir over medium heat until the honey dissolves into the water. Brush the mixture over the dough and sprinkle with sea salt.

Pop the trays into the oven and bake for 10–15 minutes or until the flatbread is thin and crunchy. Leave to cool, then break into crackers, ready to serve. Store in an airtight container.

MAKES ABOUT 20 SMALL CRACKERS OR 6 LONG CRACKERS

Honey labna
Place a sieve over a bowl. Line the sieve with a piece of muslin or a clean Chux cloth.

Put the yoghurt, honey and salt in a separate bowl. Scrape the seeds from the vanilla bean into the mixture, and stir until combined. Spoon into the sieve, gather the cloth into a loose ball and secure tightly with an elastic band. Pop the ball into the sieve over the bowl and refrigerate for 48 hours – the longer it's left, the thicker the labna will become.

MAKES ABOUT 1 CUP

HOME-MADE CRÈME FRAÎCHE
AND TOASTED CARDAMOM SUGAR (WITH PEACHES)

This is a perfect gift tray or afternoon treat when peaches are in season. Slice juicy, ripe peaches and dip into the tangy home-made crème fraîche, then sprinkle with the toasted cardamom sugar. Cardamom is my all-time favourite spice and when toasted and ground, its warm flavours are heightened to new levels of deliciousness, taking on an intense, almost warm minty aroma that is far more powerful than regular ground cardamom.

The toasted cardamom sugar is also lovely with pineapple, orange, apricot, pear, apple… I could go on. And on. For example, generously sprinkle the sugar over halved plums, dot with a little butter and roast until soft, then serve with vanilla ice cream. Or toast a really nice slice of fruit loaf, spread it with crème fraîche or ricotta and sprinkle it with cardamom sugar.

You might find it unrealistic to suggest you make crème fraîche rather than buy it. And of course, there's nothing stopping you from doing the latter. However, crème fraîche can be tricky to find for us country mice. Plus, making this otherwise expensive stuff at home is as easy as stirring a little cream and buttermilk together and leaving it on the bench for a day or two. This recipe makes a lovely thick, tangy version that will keep in the fridge for up to 2 weeks.

You can also dollop the tangy crème fraîche on fresh berries.

Ground toasted cardamom
1/3 cup (35 g) cardamom pods

Preheat the oven to 140°C (275°F). Scatter the cardamom pods over a baking tray and bake for 10 minutes or until beginning to turn dark green. Leave to cool, then transfer to a high-powered blender, food processor, spice grinder or coffee grinder and blitz as finely as possible. Pass the ground cardamom through a sieve to remove any larger pieces.

Store in an airtight container as the best ground cardamom ever, or use to make cardamom sugar.

MAKES ABOUT 1 1/2 TABLESPOONS

Toasted cardamom sugar
2 tsp ground toasted cardamom, or to taste
1/2 cup (110 g) golden caster sugar (or regular caster sugar)
A pinch of sea salt

Mix the ground toasted cardamom and sugar to taste and add the salt. Check the flavour – if it's too strong for you, add a little more sugar.

This mixture will stay potent in flavour for up to a week when stored in a jar out of direct sunlight.

MAKES ABOUT 1/2 CUP

Home-made crème fraîche
1 cup (250 ml) single (pure) cream
2 Tbsp buttermilk

Whisk the cream and buttermilk in a large jar. Place a layer of muslin or a clean Chux cloth on top and secure with twine or an elastic band, to stop bugs, dust or anything else getting into the mixture.

Leave the mixture to do its thing on the bench for 24 hours – it should thicken to the consistency of a good Greek-style yoghurt. If needed, leave it for another 24 hours. Stir well, transfer to a container with a lid and store in the fridge for up to 2 weeks.

MAKES ABOUT 1 CUP

VANILLA SALT
(WITH TOMATOES)

I discovered this wondrous condiment thanks to Renee Erickson's book, *A Boat, a Whale and a Walrus*. Her flavour combinations are a great source of inspiration to me and when she suggested making vanilla salt to sprinkle on tomatoes and poached fruits, I was smitten. A little jar of this stuff makes a great present to say thanks for having us for dinner, thanks for teaching my angel all year, and so on.

1 cup (225 g) sea salt flakes
2 vanilla beans, split lengthways

Place the sea salt in a small bowl. Scrape the vanilla seeds into the salt, and use your fingers to work them together. Divide the vanilla salt into small jars and add the empty vanilla beans (they'll keep imparting flavour). Serve with ripe tomatoes of any variety.

NOTE
For a super-delicious dessert, take another cue from Renee Erickson and serve vanilla ice cream with a sprinkle of vanilla salt and a drizzle of olive oil. (I know it sounds weird but it tastes amazing.) Make your own ice cream using the custard on page 154 and churn it in an ice cream machine, according to the manufacturer's instructions.

MAKES ABOUT 1 CUP

LIME CHILLI SALT
(WITH WATERMELON)

This chilli salt is wonderful with juicy watermelon as I've suggested here, as well as pan-fried fish, barbecued chicken or sliced peaches. It also makes a worthwhile hangover helper when sprinkled on peanut butter toast with an extra squeeze of lime!

Zest of 2 limes, peeled off in strips
1 bird's eye chilli, chopped
1 cup (225 g) sea salt flakes (pink if you can find them)

Preheat the oven to 140°C (275°F). Line a baking tray with baking paper. Put the lime zest on one half of the tray and chilli on the other. Cook for 20 minutes or until dried and beginning to curl up around the edges.

Using a spice grinder or mortar and pestle, finely chop or pound the lime zest, and then the chilli. Mix the lime zest and chilli with the sea salt and store in a jar.

MAKES ABOUT 1 CUP

COLD VANILLA
AND BUTTERMILK SOUP
(WITH RASPBERRIES)

This tangy chilled soup is a refreshing treat on a hot day. Packaged in a thermos with some fresh raspberries and Brunekager biscuits (page 107), it makes a beautiful gift.

2 egg yolks
1/3 cup (75 g) caster sugar
1 vanilla bean, split lengthways
4 cups (1 litre) buttermilk
Grated zest of 1 lemon

Beat the egg yolks and sugar together in a bowl until pale and frothy. Scrape the vanilla seeds into the yolk mixture. Add the buttermilk and lemon zest and whisk well. Cover the bowl and pop it in the fridge to chill for at least 3 hours.

MAKES ABOUT 4 CUPS

CHOCOLATE SAUCE AND SWEET DUKKAH
(WITH CHERRIES)

This dukkah is incredibly useful to have in the pantry and can jazz up pretty much anything with flavour and crunch. I sprinkle it on everything from porridge to Bircher muesli (page 193), cheesecakes, poached and fresh fruit, and pancakes with yoghurt. Here, with chocolate sauce and cherries, it makes a smart goodie box that anyone would be thrilled to find on their doorstep.

Chocolate sauce
1 cup (250 ml) single (pure) cream
1⅓ cups (200 g) chopped good-quality dark chocolate
1 Tbsp (20 g) butter

Sweet dukkah
½ cup (75 g) hazelnuts or walnuts
⅓ cup (50 g) sesame seeds
2 Tbsp poppy seeds
½ tsp coriander seeds
⅔ cup (100 g) raw unsalted pistachio nuts
½ tsp ground cardamom (see page 130 for my ground toasted cardamom)
½ tsp ground cinnamon
¼ tsp ground nutmeg
2 Tbsp soft brown sugar
A pinch of sea salt

Chocolate sauce
Heat the cream in a small saucepan over medium–high heat until just at boiling point. Remove from the heat and stir through the chocolate and butter until melted and smooth.

Store and seal in a jar or bottle in the fridge (it will need to sit at room temperature for an hour or so to soften up before serving).

MAKES ABOUT 1½ CUPS

Sweet dukkah
Preheat the oven to 180°C (350°F). Spread the hazelnuts or walnuts on a baking tray and toast for 5 minutes. Add the sesame seeds, poppy seeds and coriander seeds and continue to toast for another 5 minutes. Remove from the oven.

Combine the hazelnuts or walnuts and pistachios in a food processor or use a mortar and pestle and blitz or bash until the mixture resembles coarse breadcrumbs. Add the toasted seeds, spices, brown sugar and salt. Give it another quick blitz or bash and mix to combine, then store in a jar or airtight container.

MAKES ABOUT 1½ CUPS

Autumn

On our farm, smoko is an early lunch. Or bribery to keep everyone working just a little longer.

Smoko

Apple, fennel and pork sausage rolls ~ Quick tomato chutney
Oatcakes ~ Quince chutney ~ Blackberry and rosemary loaf

Generosity and hospitality are common themes in country cooking. I'm always amazed by the speed with which food is produced in a country kitchen as soon as someone looks hungry. A sandwich, a piece of cake or biscuits appear from nowhere and it seems like the kettle is always on.

I love this easy generosity. I love that because shops are generally a fair drive away, kitchens are well stocked and ready to whip up any manner of sustenance. And I love the tradition of smoko.

Smoko is a substantial snack and rest break in the middle of a morning or afternoon of work. Usually there's something hot to eat and a big pot of tea to share. I have a friend who lives on her family farm west of Broken Hill and every day they make enormous trays of muffins, sausage rolls and quiches for 9am smoko to feed the shearing crews who have been going since 5am.

On our farm, smoko is an early lunch. Or bribery to keep everyone working just a little longer. These sausage rolls with tomato chutney do the trick, and my oatcakes spread with some blue cheese and quince chutney are firm favourites. I also like to sweeten the deal with this moist blackberry loaf.

Quince chutney

APPLE, FENNEL AND PORK SAUSAGE ROLLS

These sausage rolls are excellent for smoko break, lunch or dinner. If serving them as a main meal, add a big salad full of peppery greens and a spicy tomato chutney like the one below. Make up a double batch of sausage rolls and freeze them (uncooked) in long logs, ready to bake from frozen, and you'll be ready to feed the hungry hordes in minutes.

1 Tbsp (20 g) butter
1 tsp fennel seeds
2 granny smith apples, cut into small pieces
1 red onion, diced
500 g (1 lb 2 oz) pork mince
1 Tbsp thyme leaves
3 sheets butter puff pastry, thawed
1 egg, lightly whisked
2 Tbsp sesame seeds
1 tsp sea salt
Quick tomato chutney (see below), to serve

Melt the butter in a heavy-based frying pan over medium–high heat. Add three-quarters of the fennel seeds and the apple pieces and cook for a few minutes or until softened. Reduce the heat to low, add the onion and cook, stirring often, for 10 minutes. Remove from the heat and allow to cool.

Preheat the oven to 200°C (400°F). Line a large baking tray with baking paper.

In a large bowl, mix the pork and thyme with the cooled apple mixture, and season with salt and pepper. Take a third of this mixture and place it on one of the thawed pastry sheets, making a sausage shape along the bottom third of the sheet. Roll as tightly as you can to create one long sausage. Repeat with the remaining pastry and pork mixture.

If you're freezing the sausage rolls at this point, wrap them in plastic wrap and pop them in the freezer. Otherwise, onwards! Using a pastry brush (or your fingers if you don't have one), brush the egg over each sausage roll. Sprinkle the sesame seeds, sea salt and remaining fennel seeds over the top.

Bake for 35–40 minutes or until the sausage rolls are golden brown. Cut into pieces and serve warm or at room temperature with the tomato chutney.

SERVES 4–6

QUICK TOMATO CHUTNEY

Chop 1 kg (2 lb 4 oz) tomatoes and 4 red onions. Seed and chop 2 bird's eye chillies (or to taste). Combine the tomato, onion and chilli in a large saucepan over medium heat. Stir in 1¼ cups (280 g) firmly packed soft brown sugar, 1 Tbsp sea salt and ⅔ cup (170 ml) apple cider vinegar. Bring to the boil and cook, stirring often (so you don't burn the base of the pan), for 40 minutes or until the chutney is thick and glossy. Divide among sterilised jars and seal. **Makes about 4 cups**

Make a double batch of these to freeze
and you'll be ready to feed the
hungry hordes in minutes.

143

OATCAKES

In my very early twenties I spent a Scottish summer working in a guesthouse on the spectacularly beautiful Isle of Mull. Every evening we served oatcakes and local stilton with pre-dinner drinks and I've loved them ever since. Especially with a slice of crunchy apple, blue cheese and a thermos of tea.

2 cups (200 g) rolled oats
1⅓ cups (200 g) plain flour
1 Tbsp soft brown sugar
1 tsp sea salt, plus extra for sprinkling
100 g (3½ oz) butter, cut into cubes

Preheat the oven to 160°C (320°F). Line two baking trays with baking paper.

Combine the oats, flour, sugar, salt and butter in the bowl of a food processor and blitz for a few seconds. Add ¼ cup (60 ml) water and blitz again until the mixture resembles coarse sand. Add 1 tablespoon of water if necessary to bring the mixture together.

Tip the dough out onto a work surface and bring together into a disc. Roll out between two pieces of baking paper until about 3 mm (⅛ inch) thick. Cut into rounds using a 5 cm (2 inch) cutter (or thereabouts). Sprinkle with sea salt and place on the baking trays. Bake for about 20 minutes or until the oatcakes are golden. Transfer to a wire rack to cool.

MAKES ABOUT 40

Great !
make w/ kids

QUINCE CHUTNEY

Quinces are one of my all-time favourite fruits and their aromatic, floral flavour really sings in this chutney. It's a perfect match for a creamy blue cheese and crumbly oatcakes.

1 kg (2 lb 4 oz) quinces
Juice of 2 lemons – about ¼ cup (60 ml)
500 g (1 lb 2 oz) caster sugar
2 Tbsp yellow mustard seeds
1 tsp ground cinnamon
3 star anise
1 tsp sea salt
1 vanilla bean, split lengthways
300 ml (10½ fl oz) apple cider vinegar
1 cup (250 ml) white wine

Halve and core the quinces, leaving the skin on, then cut into small cubes and place in a large heavy-based saucepan. Throw in three or four of the cores for extra pectin and colour. Pour in the lemon juice and 4 cups (1 litre) water. Bring to the boil, then reduce the heat and simmer for 1 hour or until the quinces are soft, stirring often so they don't catch on the pan. Drain, reserving the cooking liquid, and set aside.

Put the sugar, spices and salt in the empty saucepan. Scrape the vanilla seeds into the pan, add the vanilla bean and then pour in the vinegar, wine and reserved cooking liquid. Bring to a rolling boil, stirring every so often so the sugar dissolves. Cook for 5 minutes to reduce and intensify the syrup, then add the quinces. Boil for 40 minutes or until the quinces are very soft and the mixture is syrupy and turning a lovely blush pink colour. Discard the vanilla bean.

Transfer the chutney into sterilised jars and seal tightly, then turn the jars upside down to cool.

MAKES ABOUT 3 CUPS

BLACKBERRY AND ROSEMARY LOAF

This loaf is nutty, rich and delicious with a strong iced coffee around 3pm. Or any time. Swap the blackberries for any other seasonal fruit you like. I have also swirled Quince butter (page 199) through the batter before baking, which was delicious.

½ cup (100 g) fine semolina
1¾ cups (190 g) hazelnut meal
2 tsp baking powder
1 tsp sea salt
200 g (7 oz) unsalted butter, softened
⅔ cup (150 g) caster sugar
2 Tbsp rosemary leaves, very finely chopped
3 eggs, at room temperature
⅓ cup (95 g) Greek-style yoghurt
2 Tbsp honey
1 generous handful blackberries
1 rosemary sprig, to decorate

Preheat the oven to 180°C (350°F). Grease a 23 x 13 cm (9 x 5 inch) loaf tin and line with baking paper.

In a large bowl, combine the semolina, hazelnut meal, baking powder and sea salt.

Combine the butter, sugar and rosemary in the bowl of an electric mixer and beat until pale and fluffy. Add the eggs, one at a time, beating well after each addition. Gently fold in half the yoghurt and honey, then fold in half the dry ingredients. Repeat, folding until all the ingredients are well combined.

Spoon the batter into the loaf tin, smooth the surface and arrange the blackberries on top. Bake for 50 minutes or until crisp, golden and a skewer comes out clean. Let the loaf rest in the tin for 5 minutes, then gently turn out onto a tray to cool. Serve topped with a rosemary sprig.

SERVES 8

I like to serve this with yoghurt, honey and more blackberries.

Venison shepherd's pie

Taking comfort in the season

Honey-roasted vegetables with orangey hummus ~ Venison shepherd's pie
Fig and hazelnut cobbler ~ A big jug of custard ~ Blackberry and apple crumble

Thank goodness autumn is here. Finally there's a chill in the air, and the summer sun's
blinding glare has given way to a gentle light, a settling of the dust and an excuse to use
the oven again. It's time to dig out the soft woollen blankets and dive into crumbles and
custards, roasts and pies. This collection of recipes is an ode to all of the above, to the
reprieve autumn brings and the baking and sharing of comfort foods for cooler days.

HONEY-ROASTED VEGETABLES
WITH ORANGEY HUMMUS

1 bunch baby radishes
2 bunches baby carrots (different colours if you can find them)
1 bunch baby beetroot
Juice of 1 lemon
2 Tbsp honey
2 Tbsp olive oil
1 tsp sea salt

Orangey hummus
³/₄ cup (145 g) dried chickpeas, soaked overnight in cold water
  then cooked until tender, or 400 g (14 oz) tin chickpeas,
  rinsed and drained
¹/₃ cup (90 g) tahini
Grated zest of 1 orange
¹/₄ cup (60 ml) freshly squeezed orange juice
2 garlic cloves
1 tsp sea salt
¹/₂ tsp ground cumin

A rainbow of vegetables, roasted with a little honey, can stand alone as a fabulous main meal, especially when served on a bed of delicious hummus and alongside a peppery rocket (arugula) salad. This is also a good side dish for roasted or barbecued meats and absolutely begs for some warm Turkish bread or other flatbread.

The vegetables I used here were grown by Erika (who is pictured on page 148) and her partner Hayden. They grow organic produce from their plot at the base of the Blue Mountains. I am ever in awe of their commitment to, and love of, what they do, and you can taste that love in every crunchy carrot and radish. You can find Erika's kraut recipe on page 200.

Preheat the oven to 200°C (400°F). Line a large baking tray with baking paper.

Trim the vegetables and halve or quarter any large radishes or beetroot. Combine the vegetables on the tray and drizzle with the lemon juice, honey and olive oil. Sprinkle with the sea salt and some freshly ground black pepper and roast for 30 minutes or until the vegetables are soft and beginning to brown.

Meanwhile, to make the hummus, combine the chickpeas in a food processor with the tahini, orange zest, orange juice, garlic, sea salt and cumin. Blitz until the hummus has a lovely smooth consistency, adding a little iced water if it's too thick. Check the seasoning, adjust to taste and serve, or store in the fridge for up to a fortnight.

To serve, spread the hummus over a large plate and top with the warm roasted vegetables.

SERVES 6

VENISON SHEPHERD'S PIE

Like all good, simple fare, this pie's deliciousness is all thanks to the sum of its parts – a base of tasty soffritto, good-quality meat minced by hand and a light, fluffy potato topping. You could speed it up by skipping the long slow soffritto step and just sweating the onion, carrot and celery for 10 minutes or until soft and translucent. And you could also just buy pre-minced meat. The end result will still be lovely.

I am of course biased because we produce venison here on our farm, but truly this is the most wonderful of meats. Lean, full of delicate flavour and so easy to cook, please do try it whenever you get the opportunity. Here, venison brings an extra level of luxury to this simple, wonderful pie, but you could also stick with tradition and make this with minced lamb, or even minced beef (which is known as a cottage pie).

3 brown onions, diced
2 carrots, peeled and diced
2 celery stalks
¼ cup (60 ml) olive oil
700 g (1 lb 9 oz) venison topside
   or rump
150 g (5½ oz) butter
1 Tbsp thyme leaves
400 ml (14 fl oz) beef stock
1 Tbsp cornflour
2 Tbsp Worcestershire sauce
2 Tbsp tomato paste (concentrated
   purée)
1 kg (2 lb 4 oz) floury potatoes
¼ cup (60 ml) milk

First start the soffritto. Combine the onion, carrot, celery and olive oil in a saucepan over low heat. Cook for 2 hours, stirring every now and then, until the mixture is a thick, dark-brown paste.

Meanwhile, cut the venison into small, pea-sized pieces. Doing this by hand takes about 10 minutes, but you could ask your butcher or use a food processor or mincer if you have one.

Melt 20 g (¾ oz) of the butter in a large heavy-based saucepan over medium–high heat. Add the venison and thyme and cook, stirring often, until the venison is browned all over. Whisk together the beef stock and cornflour and add to the venison with the soffritto, Worcestershire sauce and tomato paste. Stir well, bring to a simmer and cook over low heat for 40 minutes. Season to taste.

While the meat is cooking, peel and cut the potatoes into small cubes. Place in a large saucepan and cover with cold water. Cook over high heat until the potato is completely tender when pierced with a fork. Drain and mash with 50 g (1¾ oz) of the butter and the milk.

Preheat the oven to 180°C (350°F). Transfer the meat mixture to an ovenproof dish and top with the mashed potato (I sometimes add it in clumps, which seems to help it crunch up during baking). Dot the top with the remaining butter and bake for 45 minutes or until the potato is golden and the meat is bubbling. Serve with a simple green salad.

A NOTE ON THE SOFFRITTO
Soffritto is a recipe base, usually of carrot, celery and onion cooked long and slow in olive oil, versions of which play a big part in Italian, French, Spanish and South American cooking. Although it is cooked for 2 hours in this recipe, most of that time is completely hands off and the result is an intense flavour bomb that will bring goodness to any soup, casserole, braise or pasta sauce you use it in. Make a double batch and freeze it in ice-cube trays for easy flavour access.

SERVES 6–8

FIG AND HAZELNUT COBBLER

I can't think of a more delicious dish to make and serve or give people for a cool Sunday morning in autumn. Swap the figs with any other seasonal fruit you like; poached quinces, pears or rhubarb would be gorgeous, as would stone fruit or berries. You could also serve the cobbler as a pudding with the custard from page 154.

80 g (2¾ oz) butter, melted,
   plus extra for greasing
½ cup (75 g) plain flour
½ cup (75 g) wholemeal plain flour
½ cup (110 g) golden caster sugar,
   plus a little extra for sprinkling
1½ tsp baking powder
A pinch of sea salt
½ cup (125 ml) buttermilk
2 eggs
1 tsp vanilla bean paste
Grated zest of 1 orange
8 figs, quartered
1 cup (135 g) toasted hazelnuts,
   roughly chopped
Honey, for drizzling
Greek-style yoghurt, to serve

Preheat the oven to 170°C (340°F). Use a little butter to grease a large ovenproof dish.

Whisk together the flours, sugar, baking powder and sea salt in a large bowl. In a jug, whisk together the buttermilk, melted butter, eggs, vanilla and orange zest.

Fold the wet and dry ingredients together until just combined, then pour into the dish, top with the figs and sprinkle with a little extra sugar. Bake for 25 minutes or until the batter is golden but still a little wobbly (don't overcook or it will dry out).

Sprinkle the hazelnuts over the cobbler and drizzle with a little honey. Serve warm with thick Greek-style yoghurt.

SERVES 6

A BIG JUG OF CUSTARD

Combine 1¼ cups (310 ml) milk and 1¼ cups (310 ml) single (pure) cream in a saucepan over medium–high heat. Split a vanilla bean lengthways and scrape the seeds into the pan. Add the vanilla bean and heat until the mixture is almost boiling.

Whisk ⅓ cup (75 g) caster sugar, 1 Tbsp cornflour and 6 egg yolks until pale and creamy. Splash a little of the warm milk mixture into the egg mixture and whisk again, then pour in the remaining milk mixture. Mix well, then return the whole lot to the saucepan. Stir over low heat for 5 minutes or until the custard is just about coating the back of your wooden spoon. Discard the vanilla bean, pour into a jug and store in the fridge until ready to serve.

Makes about 3 cups

BLACKBERRY AND APPLE CRUMBLE

This recipe makes more than you'll need for one crumble, and this is because I'd love you to set aside half the crumble mixture and pop it in the freezer. That means you are only ever a few unpeeled apples away from having a gorgeous crumble in the oven. Also, it makes a wonderful topping for all kinds of cakes – sprinkle a cup or so over the top of my sturdy picnic cake (page 185) before baking, for example. You can also spread it over a baking tray and bake until crunchy, then use it as a rich granola-style topping for ice cream, roasted fruit, yoghurt and fresh fruit for breakfast, and so on.

Depending on availability and taste, please go ahead and swap the blackberries with any other berry and the apple with poached quinces or stewed plums. And the hazelnuts could move aside for almonds, walnuts, pecans or a combination of all three.

Regarding what to serve crumble with, my feeling (for what it is worth) is always and only custard. Whether to serve this hot or cold has been a cause of ongoing debate in my house and we've settled it with the mandate that a hot pudding should be set down with a chilled custard and vice versa.

6 cooking apples, peeled, cored and
  thinly sliced
2 cups (260 g) blackberries
Grated zest and juice of 1 orange
2 Tbsp caster sugar

Crumble topping
280 g (10 oz) unsalted butter
2 cups (300 g) plain flour
1 cup (220 g) firmly packed soft
  brown sugar
¼ tsp ground cinnamon
A pinch of salt
¾ cup (115 g) toasted hazelnuts
1⅓ cups (135 g) rolled oats

Preheat the oven to 180°C (350°F).

For the crumble topping, combine the butter, flour, brown sugar, cinnamon, salt and hazelnuts in the bowl of a food processor and blitz for a few seconds, until just combined. (Or combine in a large bowl and work together with your fingertips until coarse and lumpy.) Add the oats and mix well. If you're freezing any of the crumble mixture, transfer it to a container or snap-lock bag now and then pop it into the freezer.

Spread the crumble mixture over a couple of baking trays and bake for 20 minutes or until just beginning to turn golden. Toss it around halfway through cooking so nothing gets stuck on the trays.

Meanwhile, prepare the fruit. Combine the apples, blackberries, orange zest, orange juice, caster sugar and 2 tablespoons water in a saucepan. Cover and cook over medium–low heat for 10 minutes, stirring halfway through, or until the fruit is tender.

Transfer the fruit mixture to an ovenproof dish – the size depends on how deep you like your crumble, but I generally use a 30 cm (12 inch) enamel roasting tin that's 5 cm (2 inches) deep. Sprinkle the roasted crumble mixture over the fruit and bake for 20 minutes.

SERVES 6–8

Out for lunch

Menu 1: *Pasta salad with olive and walnut pesto ~ Smoky zucchini and chilli hummus*
Rosemary crackers (page 129) ~ Baci di dama

Menu 2: *Crunchy fennel and apple salad ~ Triple-ginger loaf*

Menu 3: *Tomato, capsicum and pearl couscous salad ~ Christmas trail mix (page 107)*

My time working with Slow Food in Italy was such an eye-opener in terms of how we eat lunch at work. I'd just come from a busy office in Sydney where most of us would eat one-handed at our desks, barely paying attention to what we were actually ingesting, all the while staring at the computer screen. When I recounted this scenario to my Italian friends they first expressed sympathy for our sad existence, then moved to disapproval about this unsophisticated waste of a mealtime experience.

I know this isn't true of all Italian offices, but where I worked, everyone left the office at lunch for at least half an hour (and usually more like one to one and a half hours). We'd have a meal, at home or the nearby cafe, then finish with a coffee and more conversation before going back to work. And work we did – better I think, for having had such a good break.

These days I work from home, sharing the farm office with my husband, Tim. Too often we quickly throw something together before rushing back to our desks to eat. But it makes a huge difference to the afternoon's productivity if we take even 20 minutes to sit in the sun and slowly eat lunch. This menu is a reminder to myself to do that more often, and an encouragement to you to do the same. Surely we can all spare 20 minutes away from our desks to refuel. Better yet, imagine how happy it would make someone if you made them a 'not-sad desk lunch' and invited them to the park to eat with you.

PASTA SALAD WITH OLIVE AND WALNUT PESTO

This is a really tasty pasta salad that packs lots of flavour and tastes great cold. I also suggest making a double batch of the pesto because it goes beautifully with practically anything. Serve it as a dip, with barbecued meats, dolloped on top of a vegetable soup or stirred into a simple brown rice bowl with a few extra vegetables for a fast lunch.

500 g (1 lb 2 oz) wholemeal pasta spirals
2 handfuls baby English spinach
Flaked or grated parmesan cheese, to serve
Chilli flakes, to taste

Olive and walnut pesto
½ cup (90 g) green olives, pitted and roughly chopped
½ cup (60 g) walnuts, toasted and roughly chopped
2 garlic cloves, roughly chopped
1 handful mint leaves
1 Tbsp white miso paste
Juice of 1 lemon
¼ cup (60 ml) olive oil

Cook the pasta according to the packet instructions.

Meanwhile, for the pesto, combine the chopped olives and walnuts with the garlic, mint, miso paste and lemon juice in a large mortar and pestle or food processor and bash or blitz until you have a coarse paste. Loosen the pesto with the olive oil.

Drain the pasta, reserving ¼ cup (60 ml) of the cooking water. Stir the pesto through the warm pasta, adding a little of the cooking water if it looks dry. Fold the spinach through the pasta, season to taste and top with the parmesan and chilli flakes. Serve immediately or pop in the fridge for up to 2 days.

SERVES 4

SMOKY ZUCCHINI AND CHILLI HUMMUS

There is so much to love about this recipe. It's a wonderfully not-boring way to use up a glut of zucchini, and it's really versatile. Use it as a dip or give it a more prominent role as a base for sliced cherry tomatoes drizzled with olive oil, or as a bed for barbecued chicken or pan-fried fish. I also love to dollop some on top of some brown rice along with a handful of greens and some hot-smoked salmon as a super-quick grain bowl.

6 zucchini (courgettes), cut into rough chunks
⅓ cup (80 ml) olive oil
½ tsp chilli flakes
½ tsp sea salt, or to taste
1 Tbsp tahini
Juice of 1 lemon
2 Tbsp Greek-style yoghurt

Preheat the oven to 200°C (400°F). Put the zucchini chunks in a roasting tin, drizzle with half of the olive oil and sprinkle with the chilli flakes, sea salt and some freshly ground black pepper. Roast for 40 minutes or until the zucchini is soft and beginning to caramelise and darken around the edges.

Transfer the zucchini to a blender or food processor, scraping as much from the base of the tin as possible (this gives colour and flavour). Add the tahini, lemon juice and remaining olive oil and blitz until smooth. Stir in the yoghurt and season to taste. Store in the fridge for up to a week.

MAKES ABOUT 1½ CUPS

CRUNCHY FENNEL AND APPLE SALAD

Pack this gorgeous, crunchy autumn salad (pictured on page 157) with a piece of chewy baguette or sourdough to mop up the lovely dressing. Consider making a double batch of the dressing – it's lovely with any green salad.

2 fennel bulbs, trimmed
1/4 white cabbage, trimmed
2 granny smith apples
1/2 cup (75 g) hazelnuts, toasted and roughly chopped
2 Tbsp dill leaves, finely chopped

Buttermilk dressing
1/4 cup (60 ml) buttermilk
2 Tbsp Greek-style yoghurt
Juice of 1 lemon
1 tsp dijon mustard

Thinly slice the fennel, cabbage and apples (I use a mandolin). Combine with the hazelnuts and dill in a bowl.

Combine the dressing ingredients in a jar and shake well to combine.

Mix the dressing with the salad and season to taste.

SERVES 4

TOMATO, CAPSICUM AND PEARL COUSCOUS SALAD

Full of colour and flavour, this vegetarian salad is the antithesis of a sad desk lunch. Pack it up with some fresh seasonal fruit and a handful of Christmas trail mix (page 107) and you'll really be looking forward to lunchtime.

2 red capsicums (peppers)
2 yellow capsicums (peppers)
8 tomatoes, halved
Olive oil, plus extra for drizzling
Sea salt
1 1/3 cups (250 g) pearl couscous
2 cups (500 ml) boiling water
2/3 cup (100 g) crumbled feta cheese
2 Tbsp pine nuts, toasted

Dressing
1/4 cup (60 ml) red wine vinegar
1/4 cup (60 ml) olive oil
2 Tbsp sesame seeds, toasted
2 Tbsp nigella seeds
1 tsp ground cumin

Preheat the oven to 200°C (400°F). Cut the red and yellow capsicums into quarters, removing the seeds, and place on a baking tray. Put the tomato halves on another baking tray. Drizzle the vegetables with olive oil and sprinkle with sea salt. Pop the capsicums in the oven for 30 minutes, then add the tomatoes and roast for a further 20 minutes or until the capsicums are completely softened and beginning to blacken around the edges.

Meanwhile, put the couscous and boiling water in a saucepan over medium–high heat. Cook for 8 minutes or until the couscous is tender and most of the water has been absorbed. Cover the pan with a tea towel.

Mix together the dressing ingredients and season well.

Use a fork to stir the dressing through the couscous, then gently fold in the roasted capsicum and tomato. Sprinkle with the feta and toasted pine nuts. Serve immediately or store in the fridge for up to 3 days.

SERVES 4–6

Imagine how happy it would make someone if you gave them this 'not-sad desk lunch'.

VARIATION
Instead of sandwiching these together, you could melt some white, milk or dark chocolate and either dip the cookies into the chocolate or drizzle them with chocolate on the trays.

BACI DI DAMA

Baci di dama are gorgeous little hazelnut and chocolate biscuits from Piedmont, the north-western pocket of Italy that I called home for some years. The area is known for growing beautiful hazelnuts (it claims to be the home of Nutella), and every cafe and patisserie in the region sells baci di dama (ladies' kisses) by weight. I remember friends coming over to dinner with little waxed bags of baci di dama to share with coffee.

Bring a bag of these and a coffee to work for an extra nice colleague and it will make his or her day. They are a touch crumbly while still warm, so be gentle with them. Good fresh hazelnuts are the key here.

1 cup (135 g) hazelnuts, toasted and skinned
¾ cup (130 g) rice flour
2 Tbsp plain flour or gluten-free plain flour
100 g (3½ oz) chilled butter, cut into cubes
2 Tbsp ice-cold water
⅓ cup (75 g) caster sugar
½ cup (75 g) chopped dark chocolate

Using a food processor, blitz the hazelnuts into a fine meal. Add the rice flour, plain flour, butter, water and sugar. Blitz for about 10 seconds or until the mixture is just coming together. Turn out onto a work surface and bring together into a rough dough. Form the dough into a disc, wrap in plastic wrap and place in the fridge to chill for 30 minutes.

Preheat the oven to 180°C (350°F). Line two large baking trays with baking paper.

Pull out a piece of dough about the size of a marble, roll it into a ball between your hands and place on one of the trays. Repeat with the remaining dough. Bake the cookies for 10 minutes or until just golden brown. Transfer to a wire rack to cool.

Melt the chocolate in a heatproof bowl over a saucepan of simmering water. Spoon a little onto a cookie and sandwich with another cookie, then repeat with the remaining cookies.

MAKES ABOUT 20

TRIPLE-GINGER LOAF

This loaf is for my mother, Annie, who adores ginger in everything, and lots of it. It's not super sweet, but dark and almost spicy thanks to the triple ginger hit (ground, fresh and crystallised ginger) and the molasses. We love it with a scrape of butter and some tart jam but it's also great with a lemony cream cheese frosting, flying solo or toasted and topped with the lemon curd from page 244. I'd quite fancy this for dessert or a posh brunch: toast a fairly thin slice or two and serve it with a poached pear or quince half, a dollop of thick cream, a drizzle of poaching liquid and a sprinkle of Sweet dukkah (page 134).

¾ cup (110 g) plain flour
⅔ cup (100 g) wholemeal plain flour
1 tsp baking powder
2 tsp ground ginger
½ tsp ground cinnamon
½ tsp mixed spice
A good pinch of cayenne pepper
A good pinch of salt
100 g (3½ oz) butter, softened
⅓ cup (75 g) firmly packed soft brown sugar
1 Tbsp honey
3 eggs
2 Tbsp molasses
2 Tbsp boiling water
1 tsp bicarbonate of soda
¼ cup (60 ml) buttermilk
¼ cup (50 g) grated fresh ginger
½ cup (110 g) crystallised ginger, roughly chopped

Preheat the oven to 180°C (350°F). Grease a large loaf tin, about 30 cm (12 inches) long, and line with baking paper.

Sift together the flours, baking powder, spices and salt in a large bowl.

Put the butter, brown sugar and honey in the bowl of an electric mixer and beat until pale and creamy, at least 4 minutes. Add the eggs, one at a time, beating well after each addition.

In a third bowl, stir the molasses, boiling water and bicarbonate of soda together. Leave for a minute for it to froth up a bit, then pour into the butter mixture and mix for a couple of minutes.

Fold in the dry ingredients, then add the buttermilk. Mix to combine, then fold in the fresh and crystallised ginger. Spoon the batter into the tin and smooth the top, then bake for 45 minutes or until the loaf feels springy and has begun to pull away from the sides of the tin.

SERVES 8

MORE IDEAS FOR GOING OUT (OF THE OFFICE) FOR LUNCH

~ Beetroot, walnut and pomegranate dip (page 22) with sesame crackers
~ Simple harira soup (page 167)
~ Nutty sweet potato and lime soup (page 69)
~ Anna's minestrone (page 215)
~ Garlic scape and zucchini fritters (page 58)
~ Will's quinoa and cauliflower salad (page 97)
~ Lisa's frittata (page 174)
~ Sweet potato, lime and tamarind curry (page 211)
~ Comforting chicken and veggie casserole (page 176)
~ Pistachio, cardamom and rose balls (page 17)

Mind the gap

Spiced chia and smoothie puddings ~ Simple harira soup ~ Peanut butter muesli bars

The first few weeks of breastfeeding were marked – for me, at least – by crazy attacks of hunger. I'd be up at 3am feeding and all of a sudden be rocked by waves of hunger. The kind that could take out a whole fridge in its wake.

Sometimes you just need fast, filling food. Sometimes you are too tired or distracted to feed yourself properly, and it's helpful in those moments to have something filling, wholesome and tasty at hand. This minimises the possibility of eating a whole block of dodgy cooking chocolate out of desperation and means you are still giving your body the fuel it needs. So if you have a friend home with a new baby, heavy heart or recovering body, consider making them some super-filling and nutritious treats like these to keep handy.

SPICED CHIA AND SMOOTHIE PUDDINGS

Chia seeds are full of goodness and also very filling, ideal for anyone who's in need of nourishing food. Instead of topping the puddings with the blueberry smoothie, try adding Apple butter (page 198) or Rhubarb compote (page 30). You could also use berries or sliced peaches.

3 cups (750 ml) almond milk
   (page 19 or store bought) or
   cow's milk
½ cup (100 g) white chia seeds
½ tsp ground cinnamon
¼ tsp ground nutmeg
½ tsp vanilla bean paste
1 Tbsp maple syrup or honey
1 serve Blueberry, walnut, banana
   and ginger smoothie (page 92)
Sweet dukkah (page 134) and dried
   rose petals, to serve (optional)

Put the almond milk, chia seeds, cinnamon, nutmeg, vanilla and maple syrup into a jug and whisk to combine. Leave for 10 minutes so the mixture thickens up a little (the chia seeds will absorb the liquid), then divide the mixture among four small jars or glasses. Place the puddings in the fridge for 30 minutes.

Spoon the smoothie over the top of the puddings and return them to the fridge until ready to serve.

Just before serving, sprinkle the chia puddings with the dukkah and rose petals, if using.

SERVES 4

Try topping the puddings with apple butter, rhubarb compote, berries or sliced peaches.

SIMPLE HARIRA SOUP

A pared-down take on the classic Moroccan harira, which is traditionally served during Ramadan, this is a gorgeous, filling and healthy soup. I've been making it for lunch at workshops and at home for many years. You can leave out the chicken or replace it with diced lamb shoulder.

1 Tbsp (20 g) butter
1 brown onion, diced
1 tsp ground cumin
1 tsp ground turmeric
½ tsp ground cinnamon
600 g (1 lb 5 oz) chicken thigh
  fillets, chopped
2 x 400 g (14 oz) tins chopped
  tomatoes
400 g (14 oz) tin chickpeas, or
  ¾ cup (145 g) dried chickpeas,
  soaked overnight in cold water
  then cooked until tender
½ cup (100 g) red lentils
1 cup (20 g) flat-leaf parsley leaves,
  plus extra to serve
1 cup (30 g) coriander (cilantro)
  leaves, plus extra to serve
3 cups (750 ml) chicken stock
Turkish bread, to serve

Melt the butter in a heavy-based saucepan over medium–high heat. Cook the onion for 5 minutes or until soft and translucent. Add the spices and chopped chicken and cook, stirring often, for 5 minutes.

Stir in the tomatoes, chickpeas, lentils, herbs and stock. Gently simmer for about 30 minutes. Serve the soup with some warm Turkish bread and a few extra parsley and coriander leaves.

SERVES 8

PEANUT BUTTER MUESLI BARS

I made batch after batch of these when both Alice and Tom were newborns. They were my salvation and I guarded my stash jealously. Once Tim had a fencing contractor in for morning tea and they polished off half a jar at once. I came home from a shopping trip in town, starving, with a screaming baby in tow, and found the jar empty. With hindsight, I can admit my reaction was disproportionately angry.

It took me a while to come up with a muesli bar recipe that wasn't too soft and chewy, and that could hold together in a lunch box or jar and this is it. The key is using an egg white to bind the ingredients together and add some extra crunch.

2 cups (200 g) rolled oats
1 cup (160 g) almonds
1/2 cup (60 g) walnuts
1 cup (155 g) pepitas (pumpkin seeds)
1/2 cup (75 g) sesame seeds
1 cup (55 g) flaked coconut
1/2 cup (175 g) honey
1/3 cup (75 g) firmly packed soft
    brown sugar
3/4 cup (215 g) peanut butter (the
    good, natural kind if possible)
1 Tbsp coconut oil
1 large egg white, whisked until frothy
1/2 tsp sea salt
1/2 cup (40 g) wheatgerm
1 cup (170 g) raisins, dried cranberries,
    apricots or figs, roughly chopped

Preheat the oven to 160°C (320°F). Grease and line a 38 x 26 x 3 cm (15 x 10½ x 1¼ inch) cake tin with baking paper.

Combine the oats, almonds, walnuts, seeds and coconut on a baking tray and bake for about 15 minutes or until the coconut is just turning golden. Tip the mixture into a large mixing bowl.

Combine the honey, brown sugar, peanut butter and coconut oil in a small saucepan and bring just to the boil. Reduce the heat and cook, stirring often, for 5 minutes. Remove from the heat and set aside to cool for 10 minutes.

Stir the beaten egg white and salt into the honey mixture, then pour into the oat mixture, stir in the wheatgerm and dried fruit and mix well. Scrape the mixture into the cake tin and bake for 35 minutes or until golden brown. Leave to cool in the tin before cutting into bars or squares.

MAKES ABOUT 12

MORE IDEAS FOR MINDING THE GAP

~ Either of the dips on page 22, with a few snap-lock bags of carrot sticks, celery sticks and other crunchy vegetables
~ Cold soba noodle salad with trout and pickled cucumber (page 85)
~ Baked butterbeans (page 216)
~ Comforting chicken and veggie casserole (page 176)
~ A big jar of Light and crunchy honey granola (page 33)
~ Jars of Bircher muesli (page 193)
~ Raw chocolate peppermint slice (page 88)
~ Raw raspberry, orange and cashew slice (page 88)
~ Wholemeal orange and almond muffins (page 30)

I made batch after batch of these when both Alice and Tom were newborns.

Packed lunches

Lisa's frittata ~ Comforting chicken and veggie casserole with buttered rice
Granola and choc-chip cookies

Writing this book has brought about many emotional and humbling moments.
I've had a number of conversations with friends, Mum, my sister, sisters-in-law and
online community about what kinds of care packages they have received and given
in times of trouble or illness. In all of these stories I hear, over and over again,
just how generous people are in times of others' need.

One friend told me how much it meant to her family when, having just moved to
the area, she became very sick and had to spend six weeks in hospital while her husband
and three small children waited anxiously back home on the farm. Almost instantly, a
group of parents from their new school organised a meal roster. Participants were asked
to drop meals in a cool box at the school office by 3pm each day, so her husband or
whoever was collecting the kids could also pick up dinner. People they hardly knew,
teachers from the school and friends of friends kicked in and contributed everything from
casseroles to soups to pre-paid take-away dinners. Perhaps the most useful gift of all
was items to pack in school lunch boxes. Between worry for his partner, keeping the farm
on track and caring for three unsettled little people, her husband was completely
stretched. Having healthy lunch boxes sorted was a huge help.

Next time you make something for a friend who is going through a difficult time,
consider giving them a solution to that ever-present quandary: 'What on earth am
I going to put in the lunch boxes?' A simple question that seems so much more
of a headache when life is smacking you around a bit.

LISA'S FRITTATA

Lisa Darley is one half of Kurrafalls Farm, a beautiful property just 10 minutes away from us. Here, she and partner Quenten raise pastured chooks, Dorper sheep and two gorgeous children. With its layers of veggies, loads of eggs, cheese, potatoes and spinach, Lisa's frittata is one big beautiful meal in one.

My kids devour this for Sunday night dinner, so I usually make two frittatas, and freeze one in slices for school lunches. Final point in favour of this frittata: it's a great way to clean out the bottom of the fridge, so add any vegetables you find lurking in there – mushrooms, zucchini (courgettes), tomatoes or even roasted sweet potato.

2 sebago potatoes, about 400 g (14 oz)
2 Tbsp olive oil
1 red onion, chopped
70 g (2½ oz) pancetta, chopped
2¼ cups (100 g) baby English spinach
1⅔ cups (200 g) red grape tomatoes, halved
1 red capsicum (pepper), chopped
8 eggs
½ cup (125 ml) thick (double) cream
½ cup (40 g) shredded parmesan cheese
¼ cup (25 g) grated cheddar cheese
¼ cup (35 g) crumbled feta cheese

Preheat the oven to 200°C (400°F). Lightly grease a 5 cm (2 inch) deep ovenproof dish, 26 x 16 cm (10½ x 6¼ inches) or thereabouts – I often use a fairly deep, 30 cm (12 inch) ovenproof frying pan.

Put the potatoes in a small saucepan, cover with water and cook for about 15 minutes or until tender right through when pierced with a skewer or fork. Allow to cool, then thinly slice.

Meanwhile, heat the olive oil in a non-stick frying pan over medium heat. Cook the onion for 3 minutes. Add the pancetta and cook, stirring, for 3–4 minutes or until the onion is tender and the pancetta is golden. Add the spinach and cook for 1 minute or until the spinach has just wilted. Combine the onion mixture, tomatoes and capsicum in a bowl.

Arrange half the potato slices in a single layer in the prepared dish or pan and top with half the onion mixture. Repeat with the remaining potato and onion mixture.

Whisk the eggs and cream in a bowl. Gently pour the mixture over the vegetable mixture and sprinkle with the parmesan, cheddar and feta cheeses. Bake for 30–35 minutes or until the frittata is set and the top is golden. Stand for 5 minutes before slicing.

SERVES 6

My kids devour this for
Sunday night dinner.

COMFORTING CHICKEN AND VEGGIE CASSEROLE WITH BUTTERED RICE

On cold school days, when the kids need something undemanding and familiar, I pack them this nourishing casserole in thermos flasks. The flavours are simple and the texture is soft. It's basically a hug in a thermos.

¼ cup (35 g) plain flour
⅓ cup (80 ml/2½ fl oz) olive oil
1 whole chicken, cut into 8 pieces,
    or 6–8 chicken thigh pieces
1 leek, pale part only, thinly sliced
1 carrot, peeled and finely diced
1 celery stalk, finely diced
1 red capsicum (pepper), finely chopped
1 garlic clove, peeled
1 tsp thyme leaves
1 tsp sage leaves, finely chopped
1 tsp rosemary leaves, finely chopped
1 tsp sweet paprika
1 Tbsp tomato paste (concentrated purée)
400 g (14 oz) tin whole tomatoes
2 cups (500 ml) chicken stock

Buttered rice
1 cup (200 g) jasmine rice
60 g (2¼ oz) butter
A good pinch of salt

Season the flour with salt and pepper and place in a shallow bowl. Heat a little of the olive oil in a large saucepan over medium–high heat. Toss the chicken pieces in the flour and then brown, in batches, until each side has a lovely golden colour. Transfer the chicken to a plate.

Reduce the heat to medium–low, add a little more olive oil and cook the leek, carrot, celery, capsicum, garlic, thyme, sage and rosemary for 10 minutes or until soft. Stir in the paprika and tomato paste and cook for another minute. Return the chicken pieces to the pan and pour in the tomatoes and stock. Cover, turn the heat down as low as it will go and leave to cook for 1 hour or until tender.

For the buttered rice, cook the jasmine rice according to the packet instructions (I use the absorption method). Once cooked, stir through the butter and salt.

Serve the hot casserole with the buttered rice. If you're packing it in a thermos, do so while it's nice and hot – shred the chicken from the bones and mix it with the tomato sauce and vegetables on a bed of buttered rice.

SERVES 4–6

GRANOLA AND CHOC-CHIP COOKIES

These cookies are wholesome, absolutely delicious and stayers (by which I mean they last well in a jar or airtight container). I've been making them for years – I absolutely love them and hope you will too. If you're making these for kids to take to school, you might want to use a nut-free granola.

150 g (5½ oz) butter, softened
¼ cup (55 g) caster sugar
½ cup (110 g) firmly packed soft brown sugar
1 egg
1 tsp natural vanilla extract
1²/₃ cups (250 g) wholemeal plain flour
1 tsp baking powder
1 cup (125 g) granola (page 33 or store bought)
½ cup (85 g) milk chocolate chips

Preheat the oven to 180°C (350°F). Line two large baking trays with baking paper.

Combine the butter and sugars in the bowl of an electric mixer and beat until light and fluffy. Add the egg and vanilla and mix until well combined. Fold in the flour, baking powder, granola and chocolate chips.

Roll the mixture into balls about the size of a walnut and place on the trays, leaving space between them so they can spread. Flatten a little with a fork, then bake for 15 minutes or until golden. Leave to cool on a wire rack. If the cookies are a little soft in the middle for your taste, pop them back in the oven for another 5–10 minutes so they crisp up and keep well without going soggy. Store in a jar or airtight container.

MAKES ABOUT 24

MORE IDEAS FOR PACKED LUNCHES

~ *Garlic scape and zucchini fritters (page 58)*
~ *Chicken sandwiches (page 57)*
~ *Cold soba noodle salad with trout and pickled cucumber (page 85)*
~ *Honey-soy chicken legs (page 112) – delicious cold and a great lunchbox snack*
~ *Golden syrup biscuits (page 52)*
~ *Brown sugar and spice zucchini loaf (page 113)*
~ *Make the wholemeal pancakes from page 193, but make them smaller, then spread one with butter and jam or Apple butter (page 198) and sandwich with another.*

Autumn picnic by the river

Eggplant and tomato bake with crème fraîche ~ Pearl barley, beetroot and yoghurt salad
Piedmontese capsicums ~ Wholemeal apple and marmalade cake (aka the good, sturdy picnic cake)
Dark chocolate, ginger and almond clusters ~ Salted peanut and white chocolate cookies

All these recipes are good served at room temperature and all travel well,
which means they are not only perfect picnic fare but also excellent candidates
for dishes to make and give away to friends or family who might need
a 'love bomb' left on their doorstep.

This bake is rich and creamy yet full of zingy, punchy flavours.

EGGPLANT AND TOMATO BAKE
WITH CRÈME FRAÎCHE

I absolutely love this dish: it's rich and creamy yet full of zingy, punchy flavours, and takes full advantage of early autumn's abundance of tomatoes and eggplant. Delicious warm or at room temperature, you can make it in advance, then serve it with a green salad as a main or with grilled meat as a side dish. If you're cooking for vegetarians or friends who you suspect have had their fill of lasagne, give this a try. If you find crème fraîche elusive or costly, either make it yourself using the recipe on page 130, swap it for sour cream, or replace it with 250 g (9 oz) ricotta cheese mixed with 1/4 cup (25 g) grated parmesan cheese and an egg.

4 eggplant (aubergines), sliced into 1 cm (1/2 inch) rounds
2 tsp salt
2 Tbsp olive oil
1 brown onion, diced
4 garlic cloves, roughly chopped
1.5 kg (3 lb 5 oz) tomatoes, roughly chopped,
   or 3 x 400 g (14 oz) tins chopped tomatoes
1 handful basil, roughly chopped
1/4 cup (60 ml) vegetable oil
1 cup (100 g) finely grated parmesan cheese
300 g (10 1/2 oz) crème fraîche (page 130 or store bought)
Grated zest of 1 lemon
1/2 cup (30 g) fresh breadcrumbs (made from sourdough, if possible)

Put the eggplant slices in a large colander and sprinkle with the salt. Set aside for 1 hour, then rinse and pat dry with paper towel.

Preheat the oven to 180°C (350°F). Lightly grease a large ovenproof dish, approximately 30 x 20 x 8 cm (12 x 8 x 3 1/4 inches).

Heat the olive oil in a large saucepan over medium–high heat. Cook the onion until translucent (about 5 minutes), then add the garlic and cook for 1 minute. Tip in the chopped tomatoes and basil, reduce the heat and cook, stirring often, for 20 minutes.

Meanwhile, heat the vegetable oil in a large frying pan and, working in batches, fry the eggplant until soft and golden on each side, topping up with more oil if needed – there should be about 2 mm (1/16 inch) of oil in the pan at all times. This can feel like a bit of a punish, but it's the only messy part and definitely worth it!

Place a layer of eggplant in the ovenproof dish and top with a third of the tomato sauce. Sprinkle with a quarter of the parmesan and repeat so you have three layers of eggplant, tomato and parmesan. To finish, whisk together the crème fraîche, lemon zest and remaining 1/4 cup (25 g) parmesan. Spread this mixture over the top of the eggplant and tomato, then sprinkle with the breadcrumbs. Bake for 30 minutes or until the top is golden brown. Serve warm or at room temperature.

SERVES 6–8

PEARL BARLEY, BEETROOT AND YOGHURT SALAD

A really yummy, healthy and easy salad, this one is great for a picnic or buffet lunch as it sits around happily for ages and tastes great at room temperature. You can replace the beetroot with another roast vegetable if you prefer.

3 beetroot, cut into quarters
½ cup (125 ml) olive oil
1½ cups (300 g) pearl barley
6 cups (1.5 litres) boiling water
2 Tbsp apple cider vinegar
Grated zest and juice of 1 lemon
¼ cup (40 g) sunflower seeds
¼ cup (40 g) pine nuts
1 bunch dill, finely chopped
1 cup (260 g) Greek-style yoghurt

Preheat the oven to 200°C (400°F). Put the beetroot quarters on a baking tray, drizzle with a little of the olive oil and sprinkle with salt and pepper. Roast for 40 minutes or until tender.

Meanwhile, combine the barley and 2 tablespoons of the olive oil in a large saucepan over medium–high heat. Toast, stirring often, for 10 minutes. Pour in the boiling water and boil until tender, about 15 minutes.

Mix together the remaining olive oil, vinegar, lemon zest and lemon juice and season to taste.

Put the sunflower seeds and pine nuts in a dry frying pan and toast over medium heat, tossing occasionally, for 2 minutes or until golden.

As soon as you drain the barley, tip it into a large bowl and mix in the dressing. Leave to cool for a few minutes, then mix in the sunflower seeds, pine nuts and dill. Top with the roasted beetroot (even better if it's still warm) and yoghurt, and season to taste.

SERVES 6

PIEDMONTESE CAPSICUMS

These capsicum boats appear on antipasto plates all over Italy. They're best eaten at room temperature, which makes them perfect for picnics. I pack them on a bed of salad leaves and by the time we've arrived, the capsicum's juices have made a lovely dressing: win–win. They're also a brilliant make-ahead side dish for barbecues and are especially good with the tonnato sauce from page 76. If you have any leftovers, they make a great pasta sauce when chopped finely and tossed about in a hot frying pan for 5 minutes.

4 red capsicums (peppers), halved and seeded
4 tomatoes, halved lengthways
8 anchovy fillets, drained and finely chopped
4 garlic cloves, finely chopped
2 Tbsp capers, rinsed and chopped
2 Tbsp olive oil
1 Tbsp balsamic vinegar
Mixed salad leaves, to serve
1 handful basil leaves

Preheat the oven to 180°C (350°F). Lightly oil a large ovenproof dish. Add the capsicum halves, cut side up and well spaced, then place a tomato half, cut side up, inside each capsicum half.

Combine the anchovies, garlic and capers. Scatter over the tomato halves, then drizzle with the oil and vinegar. Bake for 45 minutes or until the capsicums and tomatoes are soft and tender.

Put the salad leaves and basil on a platter and top with the capsicums and all their beautiful juices.

SERVES 6–8

Both these are great at room temperature, making them perfect to take on a picnic.

WHOLEMEAL APPLE AND MARMALADE CAKE
(AKA THE GOOD, STURDY PICNIC CAKE)

If this cake were a woman, she'd wear sensible shoes. She'd be a reliable, fun, and self-deprecating sort of Chummy/Miranda Hart character. She wouldn't mind if you burnt her bottom, and she'd be a good sport about being transported over rough paddocks for a picnic and maybe even dropped, in which case she'd mostly hold her shape and taste great, even if she looked like a mess. She can also take any fruit you throw at her (within reason), plus she lasts for ages and is easy to make.

1 cup (100 g) almond meal (using freshly roasted, ground almonds makes a big difference)

1¼ cups (185 g) wholemeal plain flour

2 tsp baking powder

½ tsp ground cinnamon

½ tsp ground allspice

A pinch of salt

200 g (7 oz) butter, softened

¾ cup (165 g) firmly packed soft brown sugar

3 eggs, at room temperature

3 apples, cut into small chunks (I don't bother peeling them, but go ahead if you prefer)

½ cup (75 g) dried currants or raisins

¾ cup (250 g) marmalade

¼ cup (50 g) demerara sugar

Preheat the oven to 160°C (320°F). Grease a 23–24 cm (9–9½ inch) spring-form cake tin and line with baking paper.

Combine the almond meal, flour, baking powder, spices and salt in a bowl and whisk to combine and get rid of any lumps.

In the bowl of an electric mixer with a paddle attachment, cream the butter and brown sugar together for 5 minutes or until pale and fluffy. Add the eggs, one at a time, beating well after each addition. Fold in the flour mixture, then stir in the apple chunks and currants or raisins. Fold in the marmalade.

Transfer the batter to the tin, smooth the top and sprinkle with the demerara sugar. Bake for 1 hour or until the cake is just pulling away from the side of the tin and feels slightly firm to the touch. Leave to cool in the tin.

NOTE
Do wait until the cake has cooled down before moving it around too much. Any cake fresh out of the oven is going to crumble or crack if you try to get it out of the tin while still warm.

SERVES 8

All this cake asks is to be served with a thermos of strong tea.

DARK CHOCOLATE, GINGER AND ALMOND CLUSTERS

These are so easy they're hardly a recipe, but so delicious you really should give them a go. A great dessert for picnics (keep them in a cool box or chiller bag, though) and dinner parties when you can't stand plating up another course and all that extra washing up. Just pop them on a plate with a little fresh fruit and maybe some nougat or Turkish delight. I think that's all people want after a big meal – something sweet to nibble on with their last glass of wine (or two). They're also really yummy with a sprinkle of Sweet dukkah (page 134).

1 cup (150 g) chopped best-quality dark chocolate
1 cup (125 g) slivered almonds, toasted
1/2 cup (95 g) stem ginger, roughly chopped

Line a baking tray with baking paper.

Melt the chocolate in a glass bowl over a saucepan of simmering water (or however you prefer to melt chocolate). Once melted, let the chocolate cool a little, then stir in the almonds and ginger.

Scoop a tablespoon of the chocolate mixture onto the tray, keeping it in a nice round mound. Repeat with the remaining mixture. Pop in the fridge for at least an hour before serving.

NOTE
Variations to this recipe are endless, but here are a couple of ideas: swap the slivered almonds with hazelnuts and the ginger with dried figs; or swap the almonds with pistachios and the ginger with chopped Turkish delight.

MAKES ABOUT 15

SALTED PEANUT AND WHITE CHOCOLATE COOKIES

Here's one for the salty/sweet lovers. These are a gorgeous combination of salty peanuts and creamy white chocolate bound up in a crunchy, buttery biscuit, perfect with a morning coffee and also excellent crumbled over vanilla ice cream. One of the wonderful people who tested recipes for this book, the lovely Viktorija from Lithuania, said she made these without the caster sugar and they were the perfect sweetness for her taste. Feel free to do the same if your sweet tooth isn't perhaps as bad as my family's.

1 cup (150 g) plain flour
1/2 tsp baking powder
125 g (4 1/2 oz) unsalted butter, softened
1/2 cup (140 g) peanut butter
1/2 cup (110 g) firmly packed soft brown sugar
1/4 cup (55 g) caster sugar
1 egg
1 tsp natural vanilla extract
1/2 cup (80 g) salted peanuts
1 cup (140 g) white chocolate pieces
Vanilla salt (page 133) or regular sea salt, for sprinkling

Preheat the oven to 180°C (350°F). Line two baking trays with baking paper.

Sift together the flour and baking powder and set aside. Cream the butter, peanut butter and sugars together until pale and fluffy. Add the egg and vanilla and beat to combine. Fold in the peanuts and white chocolate, then fold in the flour and baking powder.

Roll a walnut-sized piece of dough into a ball and place on a tray. Repeat with the remaining mixture. Use the tines of a fork to gently press each ball down, then sprinkle with the vanilla salt or regular sea salt.

Bake the cookies for 10–12 minutes or until golden brown. Let them cool on a wire rack, then transfer to an airtight container.

MAKES ABOUT 12–16

Happy campers

Simple chicken and chorizo paella ~ Bircher muesli ~ Wholemeal pancakes
Salted caramel sauce for everything ~ Tom's chocolate cake

My love of camping blossomed only recently, around the time we took
ownership of a 1970s pop-up trailer that we all adore. It features a proper double
mattress, a little annexe for a couple of swags and a basic outdoor kitchen,
and it's by far and away the least slick set up in any camping ground.

Even though there's quite a bit of preparation involved in getting packed up and
on the road (both at the beginning and end of any camping trip), there's also nothing
quite like that first beer or glass of bubbles sitting around an open fire. Our camping
food is fairly simple but tasty and generally well received, so I go with the old 'if it ain't
broke...' theory. Lunch is generally wraps or sandwiches and dinner is a big paella,
but it's camping breakfast where I really get carried away. And we always take
a big slab of Tom's chocolate cake for morning tea or after lunch.

My love of camping blossomed
when we took ownership of a
1970s pop-up trailer.

SIMPLE CHICKEN AND CHORIZO PAELLA

I fall back on this recipe every time I go to make paella because it's always such a hit. Kids love it, teenagers inhale it and it makes adults happy too. Plus, if you have a nice big pan, this is an excellent and easy way to feed a large group. You can, of course, halve or even quarter the quantities below and cook it in a frying pan on the stove – hardly authentic, but neither is the recipe. Any leftovers can be formed into patties and fried as little rice cakes.

When I'm making this dish for camping or a picnic, I prepare the stock before we leave and keep it hot in a big thermos, ready to pour in when the time's right.

3 x 400 g (14 oz) tins whole peeled tomatoes
⅓ cup (90 g) tomato paste (concentrated purée)
¼ cup (25 g) smoked paprika
1 tsp sea salt and a good grinding of fresh black pepper
¼ cup (10 g) finely chopped rosemary
¼ cup (10 g) finely chopped sage
A good pinch of saffron threads (or more if funds allow!)
8 cups (2 litres) chicken stock
¼ cup (60 ml) olive oil
4 chorizo sausages, cut into 1 cm (½ inch) discs
5 garlic cloves, squashed with the flat side of a knife
800 g (1 lb 12 oz) skinless chicken thigh fillets, cut into 3 cm (1¼ inch) cubes
1 kg (2 lb 4 oz) calasparra rice (or at a pinch, any risotto rice)
2 cups (280 g) frozen peas
A couple of handfuls of roughly chopped flat-leaf parsley
3 lemons, quartered
1 baguette, sliced
Sliced fresh chilli or chilli flakes, to serve (optional)

Start by making the stock – this is where the flavour really comes from and by making it in advance, you cut out a fair few steps when it comes to paella time. In a large saucepan, combine the tomatoes, tomato paste, paprika, salt and pepper, herbs, saffron and chicken stock. Stir well and bring to the boil, then reduce the heat and simmer for a good 30 minutes. Check for seasoning – the stock should be richly flavoured and aromatic.

When ready to cook, place a paella pan over high heat and add the olive oil. Cook the chorizo, garlic and chicken for about 5 minutes, until the chicken is browned on the edges but only half cooked. Add the rice and stir for a couple of minutes. Pour in the tomato stock, reduce the heat to medium–low and leave to cook for about 10 minutes, without stirring. Top up the liquid with water if necessary and check the rice. If it's still crunchy, keep cooking and top up with a little more water if it looks like it's drying out. Try not to stir it much because you want a nice 'crust' to develop on the bottom of the pan. The rice should be tender with just the slightest crunch. Once it reaches that point, add the peas and a little more water if necessary (you don't want the paella to be dry at all). Cook for a few more minutes or until the peas are bright green.

Serve the hot paella with the parsley, a bunch of lemon wedges and the sliced baguette. I also put a dish of chilli on the side for the heat seekers.

SERVES 12–14

BIRCHER MUESLI

This is the best possible camping breakfast – it's all portioned up and ready to eat, and it's completely delicious and filling.

1 granny smith apple (unpeeled), grated
1 1/2 cups (150 g) rolled oats
1/4 cup (50 g) chia seeds
1/2 cup (125 ml) apple juice
1 cup (260 g) plain yoghurt
A pinch of ground cinnamon
Poached apricots (page 99), to serve

Mix the grated apple, oats, chia seeds, apple juice, yoghurt and cinnamon together. Divide among jars, cover and place in the fridge overnight.

Serve the muesli with the poached apricots or your choice of toppings.

TOPPING IDEAS
~ extra yoghurt or milk
~ fresh berries or other fruit
~ poached apples or quinces
~ Rhubarb compote (page 30)
~ toasted and roughly chopped nuts
~ Sweet dukkah (page 134)
~ a sprinkling of brown sugar
~ a drizzle of honey or maple syrup

SERVES 4

WHOLEMEAL PANCAKES

These pancakes are a big hit whether camping or at home. If you are considering the former, I suggest you make up the batter back at the ranch, then transfer it to a large plastic piping bag and seal the ends. Store it in the cool box or chiller bag and then, when it's breakfast time, just snip off the end and pipe straight into a hot, buttered frying pan.

1 cup (150 g) wholemeal plain flour
2 tsp baking powder
1 cup (250 ml) milk
1 egg
Grated zest of 1 orange
2 Tbsp caster sugar
Butter, for cooking

Combine all the ingredients in a small bowl and whisk until well combined. Store in the fridge until needed.

When ready to cook the pancakes, melt a knob of butter in a frying pan over medium heat. Cook a few tablespoons of batter at a time, cooking for a minute or so on each side. Flip once bubbles appear on the surface of the pancakes.

Serve the pancakes with poached fruit (pictured here is the Rhubarb compote from page 30), fresh fruit, caramel sauce, maple syrup and bacon or the classic lemon and sugar.

SERVES 6–8

Carry the pancake batter in a piping bag, then snip off the end and pipe straight into the frying pan.

SALTED CARAMEL SAUCE FOR EVERYTHING

This is one for my dad, who is absolutely mad for a good caramel sauce. The last time we went camping I packed a jar of this and we had it on pancakes, shaken up in a jar full of ice and milk (plus a shot of cold-brewed coffee for Tim and me), and poured over ice cream. It lasts for ages and makes a great gift. And it tastes amazing. If you're serving it as a topping, consider finishing off with a sprinkle of Vanilla salt (page 133).

You'll find the sauce thickens up quite a lot in the fridge. To soften it, just place the jar in a bowl of hot water and give it a quick zap in the microwave or transfer it to a saucepan and gently warm the sauce until it loosens up.

1³/₄ cups (390 g) caster sugar
170 g (5³/₄ oz) unsalted butter, cut into cubes
1 cup (250 ml) single (pure) cream
Seeds from 1 vanilla bean
1 tsp sea salt

Put the sugar in a saucepan over medium–high heat and cook, stirring often, until it melts into a smooth caramel (watch it carefully towards the end because it can go from perfectly golden to burnt in the blink of an eye). As soon as the sugar is completely melted and smooth, add the butter and whisk until it has melted into a smooth sauce.

Remove the pan from the heat. Whisk in the cream, vanilla seeds and salt. Return to the heat and bring to the boil. Cook, stirring often, for 5 minutes, then remove from the heat and divide among jars. Store in the fridge for up to a month.

MAKES ABOUT 2 CUPS

TOM'S CHOCOLATE CAKE

This cake is my son Tom's all-time favourite and he's not alone – I've found kids love this for its mellow flavour and soft, springy texture. I love it because it takes all of 5 minutes to throw together. Super simple. Super easy. I always take this cake camping, to picnics, sports days, etc., and it disappears in seconds.

1¹/₂ cups (225 g) self-raising flour
¹/₄ cup (30 g) cocoa powder
1¹/₄ cups (275 g) caster sugar
3 eggs, at room temperature
125 g (4¹/₂ oz) butter, softened and cut into cubes
¹/₂ cup (125 ml) milk
1 tsp vanilla bean paste

Chocolate icing

1 cup (160 g) icing sugar
2 Tbsp cocoa powder
50 g (1³/₄ oz) butter, softened
2 Tbsp milk
Sprinkles, to decorate

Preheat the oven to 180°C (350°F). Grease and line a 20 cm (8 inch) square cake tin with baking paper.

Combine all the ingredients in the bowl of an electric mixer and beat for 5 minutes. Spoon into the cake tin and bake for 30 minutes or until a skewer comes out clean. Let the cake cool in the tin for about 5 minutes before turning out to cool completely on a wire rack.

For the icing, sift the icing sugar and cocoa into a small bowl. Add the butter and milk and whisk until smooth (or use an electric mixer). Spread the icing over the cake and top with the sprinkles.

VARIATION
Leave out the cocoa (make up the weight in extra flour) and instead add the grated zest of a lemon or a generous teaspoon of mixed spice.

SERVES 6–8

Set up an outdoor kitchen and
bring together some friends
for a day of preserving.

Autumn preserving

Apple butter ~ Buttermilk scones ~ Quince butter
Erika's cabbage and caraway kraut ~ Roasted tomato passata

Autumn is the most generous of seasons – from pomme fruits in the orchard (apples, pears and quinces), to gluts of tomatoes in the garden and the end of summer's berries, figs and plums. So it follows that this is the time of year to set aside a day or so, bring together some friends and put away this goodness for the leaner winter and early spring months.

I know that preserving and pickling and bottling can be a messy business, especially if, like me, you have a small house and kitchen that gets very hot and sticky very quickly. Here's a tip I've adopted recently from a friend: head to your local camping shop and buy a cheap gas burner ring, then set up a trestle in the garden and do all your chopping, cooking and preserving outdoors. You know how they say that food tastes better outside? Well, I think food is also more fun to make outside, especially when preserving.

APPLE BUTTER

If you haven't tried apple butter, I recommend you give it a try. It's absolutely delicious and when you make it your kitchen smells amazing and you can almost imagine you are Diane Keaton in *Baby Boom*. All that will be missing is Sam Shepard walking through the door with that smile.

Apple butter is gorgeous with scones, on pancakes, sandwiched with cream between a sponge cake, over toast or even whizzed up with ice-cold milk for an apple shake. I particularly like it with a dollop of whipped cream and buttermilk scones.

8 large cooking apples (I use tart granny smith apples)
2 tsp lemon juice
2 Tbsp caster sugar
1/2 tsp ground cinnamon

Peel, core and quarter the apples, then place in an ovenproof saucepan. Add 1/2 cup (125 ml) water, the lemon juice, sugar and cinnamon. Cook over medium heat, stirring every now and then, for 30 minutes or until the apples have collapsed into a soft mush.

Preheat the oven to 150°C (300°F).

Transfer the apple mixture to a food processor and blitz until smooth. Return to the pan and cover with a lid or foil. Place in the oven for 1 hour, stirring halfway through to make sure the mixture doesn't catch on the bottom. Transfer the apple butter to jars and seal. Keep in the fridge for up to a month.

MAKES ABOUT 2 CUPS

BUTTERMILK SCONES

These buttermilk scones are rather rich and beautifully fluffy. They're absolutely delicious with the classic jam and cream combo, but especially good with a little quince or apple butter and perhaps a dollop of crème fraîche or yoghurt to cut through the richness.

2¾ cups (410 g) plain flour, plus extra for dusting
1/2 cup (110 g) caster sugar, plus extra for sprinkling
1/2 cup (100 g) soft brown sugar
2 Tbsp baking powder
1 tsp bicarbonate of soda
A good pinch of sea salt
250 g (9 oz) unsalted butter, cubed
1 cup (250 ml) buttermilk
1 egg
1/4 cup (60 ml) single (pure) cream

Combine the flour, caster sugar, brown sugar, baking powder, bicarbonate of soda and salt in the bowl of a food processor. Add the butter and blitz until the mixture just resembles coarse breadcrumbs. Pour in the buttermilk and blitz again for just a second, so that everything is barely combined.

Turn the mixture out onto a lightly floured surface and, working quickly, bring it together into a dough. Press the dough out until it's about 2 cm (¾ inch) thick. Use a 6 cm (2½ inch) cutter or sharp knife to cut the dough into rounds or triangles. Place on a baking tray lined with baking paper, then cover and place in the freezer for at least an hour.

Preheat the oven to 180°C (350°F). Whisk the egg and cream together to make an egg wash. Generously brush the scones with the egg wash and sprinkle with caster sugar, then cook in the oven for 20 minutes or until golden.

MAKES 8–10

QUINCE BUTTER

Quinces are my favourite fruit. Every autumn, I pick and poach every last one not only from the tree in our orchard but also the wild quince tree that grows in a paddock nearby. I horrify my children by jumping a fence to get to this tree every April. For years I'd drive past and watch the birds eat every last quince, so now I indulge in a little light trespassing and pick a basket, and the sky hasn't fallen in yet.

The idea of a quince butter is simple: peel, chop, poach or stew the fruit, then purée and roast in the oven to thicken up. The result is a smooth, brightly coloured and intensely flavoured butter-free butter. Use it wherever you'd reach for lemon curd or similar. I think it's amazing spread on sourdough toast with mellow, creamy ricotta, but I also enjoy it on top of yoghurt, or stir it through a vanilla custard and then freeze it for quince ice cream.

The extra nice thing about making a batch of quince butter is that when you give it away, people get super excited. I think that's probably because they've never had it before, the colour and flavour are insanely good, and they can feel the love you put into making it.

4–6 quinces
2 cups (440 g) sugar
Juice of 1 lemon
1 Tbsp vanilla bean paste
1 cinnamon stick

First you need to poach the quinces. Start by preheating the oven to 150°C (300°F).

Peel, core and quarter the quinces, reserving the cores.

Combine the sugar, lemon juice, vanilla bean paste and cinnamon in a saucepan and bring to the boil. Stir over medium heat until the sugar has dissolved, then simmer for a few minutes.

Meanwhile, arrange the quince pieces in a deep roasting tin in a single layer. Don't worry if they colour a little – this won't affect the end result. Tie the cores together in a piece of muslin and add it to the tin (I never seem to have any muslin on hand, so I just scatter a few cores over the top of the quinces then fish them out later). The cores will add colour and pectin to the fruit while cooking.

Pour the sugar syrup over the quinces and cover tightly with foil. Place in the oven for 3–4 hours or until the quinces have turned a ruby-red colour and are deliciously aromatic. Remove and discard the cores and cinnamon stick.

Let the quinces cool a little, then tip them into a food processor, syrup and all, and blitz until really smooth. Pour the puréed quince back into the roasting tin and return (uncovered) to the oven for 1 hour. This will really thicken things up nicely and intensify the flavour, too. Stir every 20 minutes to make sure the bottom doesn't burn, then transfer the quince butter to jars and seal. Keep in the fridge for up to a month.

MAKES ABOUT 2 CUPS

ERIKA'S CABBAGE AND CARAWAY KRAUT

Erika Watson of Epicurean Harvest is a friend and regular guest at my workshops. With partner Hayden Druce, she grows superb produce on their small plot in the Blue Mountains. She has a wealth of knowledge on preserving and storing seasonal excess, and this is her recipe.

Kraut is one of the simplest fermented foods around – basically cabbage leaves and salt become kraut through the process of lactic acid fermentation. By massaging the cabbage with salt, the beneficial bacteria on the surface converts sugars in the cabbage into lactic acid. This, in turn, halts the growth of harmful bacteria and creates a delicious cocktail of vitamins, enzymes and super-friendly bacteria, all of which are great for the digestive system.

If you are new to the world of fermented foods, kraut is a great place to start. It's a simple process for which you need no special equipment – just a big jar, salt and a little time. If you have a friend who has been unwell, taking rounds of antibiotics and such, a jar of kraut will be a welcome present, not only delicious but so healthy, too.

1 large savoy cabbage
3 tsp salt
1 Tbsp caraway seeds

THINGS TO DO WITH KRAUT

~ Start with the classic – pile atop a sandwich of rye bread with pastrami.
~ Dollop a tablespoon or so on top of a winter minestrone to add tang and crunch.
~ Use it as a bed for a nice fried or softly poached egg – break the egg into the kraut and stir it through, then serve with toasted sourdough.
~ Bake a potato or sweet potato in its skin, then cut open and pile in sour cream and kraut. A super-filling, yummy and healthy lunch or dinner.
~ Make up a big bowl of brown rice, veggies, nuts and maybe a fried egg, then finish with a good dollop of kraut.

Remove about five or six outer leaves from the cabbage and set aside for later. Using a large sharp knife, finely chop the whole cabbage, removing the core. Measure 13 cups (1 kg) chopped cabbage into a large bowl and add the salt and caraway seeds.

Either with a heavy pestle or your fists, pound, grab, squeeze and rub the cabbage until it's covered by its own juices that are produced by all that pounding and squeezing. Set aside for 10 minutes for the cabbage to soften, then bash and squeeze again for a few more minutes. The aim is to create enough juices to cover the cabbage once it's packed. At this point, transfer the cabbage to a wide-mouthed jar (wide enough for your fist to fit through). Push the pounded cabbage really firmly to the bottom of the jar so that the juices sit about 2.5 cm (1 inch) over the surface of the cabbage. (I use the pestle from my mortar and pestle.)

Take the reserved cabbage leaves and push them down on top of the cabbage, so they are also sitting under the liquid, acting as 'leaf seals'. Place a weight on top of the leaves, push down and seal with a lid. (I use a jar filled with water, which fits through the big jar's opening.)

Leave the cabbage to stand out of direct sunlight or covered with a tea towel for 10–14 days, depending on the time of year (in warmer weather, the fermentation process usually takes about 10 days, but it takes longer in colder weather).

Remove the weight, pour off the liquid and discard the cabbage leaf seals. (Sometimes these leaves become infected with airborne fungi or bacteria, but don't worry – they're there to protect the kraut below.) Fork the kraut into smaller jars and store in the fridge.

MAKES 1 BIG JAR

ROASTED TOMATO PASSATA

This passata is a simple enough recipe but it produces a sauce of such deep flavour that I hope you'll make it often. Roasting your tomatoes and then puréeing and bottling them is the easiest and arguably the best way to preserve seasonal gluts of this glorious fruit (no peeling, no fiddling). Even better, gather a few friends on an autumn morning and get everyone to bring one thing: a box of tomatoes, all the jars, the garlic and oil, and set aside a few hours to chop, roast, chat, bottle and drink tea.

5 kg (11 lb) vine-ripened tomatoes,
    cut into chunks
6 brown onions, cut into eighths
1 garlic bulb, cloves separated
¼ cup (60 ml) olive oil
1 tsp sea salt
½ tsp chilli flakes

Preheat the oven to 180°C (350°F). Divide all the ingredients among a few big roasting tins and toss to combine. Roast for 45 minutes or until the tomatoes and onions are completely softened and cooked through.

Remove the garlic and squeeze the roasted pulp into the roasting tins. Transfer the mixture in batches to a blender or food processor and blitz to a smooth sauce. Pour into sterilised bottles or jars and seal tightly.

You can store the bottles of passata in the fridge for up to a month, or heat preserve them so they last you right through winter. If you have a Fowlers preserving unit, follow the instructions that came with it. If you're using a stockpot, line the base with a folded tea towel, place the bottles on top and tuck a few tea towels between them so they don't clink together and break when the water boils. Bring to the boil, then reduce the heat a little and cook for 1 hour (you may need to top up the water every now and then).

Carefully remove the bottles from the preserving unit or pot and wipe down. Store in a cool dark place.

MAKES ABOUT 4 LITRES (140 FL OZ)

IDEAS FOR USING TOMATO PASSATA

~ Give away a bottle with a nice packet of pasta and a hunk of cheese.
~ Use it as a pizza sauce.
~ Pour over meatballs, chicken thigh pieces or cannelloni stuffed with ricotta and spinach, and bake.
~ Thin out with a good stock, season with salt and pepper and serve as a super-tasty tomato soup.
~ Add to a winter minestrone for some bright summer flavour.

Winter

Dahl for your darlings

Oven-roasted chicken curry ~ Simple vegetable dahl
Sweet potato, lime and tamarind curry

Oh, dahl; equal parts delicious, healthy, cheap and easy to make, dahl ticks every box. And even though this little selection of recipes only features one dahl proper, all three recipes would be perfect to make and give to someone needing warming nourishment. Together they form a fantastic feast but each one also stands alone as a meal, perhaps with some steamed white or brown rice.

OVEN-ROASTED CHICKEN CURRY

This grounding, warming curry is a meal in itself, with the split peas adding sustenance to keep you feeling full. I make it fairly mild so that everyone can enjoy it, then add a good sprinkle of fresh or dried chilli to mine at the table, along with a dollop of yoghurt. I think cooking this in the oven rather than on the stovetop produces a far richer, thicker curry, but you could take the stovetop option. Just keep the temperature low and the lid slightly off. The spice paste is worth having on hand in the fridge – simply rub it over chicken or lamb before barbecuing, or use it as a marinade.

2 Tbsp coconut oil

2 brown onions, diced

700 g (1 lb 9 oz) skinless chicken thigh fillets, cut into 3 cm (1¼ inch) pieces

½ cup (130 g) Greek-style yoghurt, plus extra to serve

2 Tbsp tomato paste (concentrated purée)

680 g (1 lb 8 oz) jar tomato passata (page 203 or store bought)

3 cups (750 ml) chicken stock

1 cup (205 g) chana dahl (split yellow lentils), soaked in cold water for at least 1 hour

2 handfuls English spinach

Toasted slivered almonds, to serve

Steamed rice, to serve

Spice paste

5 green cardamom pods

2 cloves

1 cinnamon stick

4 black peppercorns

4 garlic cloves, peeled

1 thumb-sized piece ginger, roughly chopped

1 thumb-sized piece turmeric, roughly chopped, or 1 tsp ground turmeric

1 Tbsp ground cumin

1 tsp ground coriander

A good pinch of chilli flakes, or to taste

2 Tbsp coconut oil

For the spice paste, combine the cardamom pods, cloves, cinnamon stick and peppercorns in a dry frying pan and toast for a few minutes or until fragrant. Transfer to a food processor, spice grinder or mortar and pestle and bash/blitz until well ground. Add the garlic, ginger, turmeric, cumin, coriander, chilli and coconut oil and bash/blitz again until combined.

Preheat the oven to 130°C (250°F). Heat the coconut oil in a large ovenproof saucepan or flameproof casserole dish over medium heat. Cook the onion for 7–10 minutes or until soft and translucent. Add the spice paste and cook, stirring constantly, for a few minutes. Bump up the heat to high, add the chicken and cook for 3–4 minutes to seal.

Add 1 tablespoon of the yoghurt, stirring well so all the flavours mix together and the yoghurt dries somewhat, then repeat with another tablespoon of yoghurt and another until it's all incorporated. Stir in the tomato paste and cook for another minute.

Add the passata and stir until the chicken is well coated in the spiced yoghurt mixture. Cook for 5 minutes, then pour in the stock and chana dahl and stir well. Transfer to the oven and cook for 3 hours, stirring every now and then so it doesn't stick to the bottom of the pan.

Stir in the spinach and serve the curry with slivered almonds, yoghurt and steamed rice.

SERVES 6

SIMPLE VEGETABLE DAHL

There are countless variations of dahl; this is mine – easy, mellow and tasty. Serve it with steamed brown rice and/or naan, a dollop of yoghurt or just on its own. I add a good sprinkle of chilli and a squeeze of lime or lemon juice.

1 Tbsp coconut oil, ghee or olive oil
1 brown onion, diced
1 cup (205 g) red lentils
1 Tbsp ground cumin
1 Tbsp ground turmeric
1 Tbsp garam masala
3 garlic cloves, finely chopped
4 cm (1 1/2 inch) piece ginger, peeled
   and finely chopped
1 bunch coriander (cilantro)
1 carrot, finely diced
2 celery stalks, finely chopped
4 cups (1 litre) water or stock

Heat the oil in a large saucepan over medium–high heat. Cook the onion, stirring, for a few minutes, then add the lentils, spices, garlic and ginger. Finely chop the coriander stalks and add these to the pan, along with most of the leaves (save some to garnish). Cook, stirring often, for about 10 minutes.

Add the carrot and celery and cook for a few minutes more. Pour in the water or stock, then reduce the heat and cook for 45 minutes or until the vegetables have softened completely and the lentils are tender. Add more water or stock if you feel like the dahl needs to loosen up a bit. Serve garnished with the reserved coriander leaves.

SERVES 6–8

SWEET POTATO, LIME AND TAMARIND CURRY

This curry is influenced by one of Anna Jones's recipes in her wonderful book, *A Modern Way to Cook*. I'm an enormous fan of this British food writer and her recipes are on high rotation in our house. Fresh but warming at the same time, it's a gorgeous dish. One of the army of recipe testers that I enlisted to help with this book suggested adding a cup of red lentils with the sweet potato. She also stirred through a few handfuls of greens right at the end, which is a great idea – thanks, Rachel!

1 Tbsp coconut oil or vegetable oil
1 brown onion, diced
1 bunch coriander (cilantro)
2 garlic cloves, finely chopped
3 cm (1 1/4 inch) piece ginger, peeled and
   finely chopped
600 g (1 lb 5 oz) sweet potato, peeled
   and cut into 3 cm (1 1/4 inch) cubes
1 tsp mustard seeds
2 x 400 g (14 oz) tins chopped tomatoes
2 x 400 g (14 oz) tins coconut milk
2 Tbsp tamarind paste
Juice of 1 lime
1 tsp soft brown sugar
Steamed brown rice, to serve

Heat the oil in a large flameproof casserole dish or saucepan over medium–high heat. Cook the onion, stirring often, for 5 minutes. Snip the leaves from the coriander and thinly slice the stalks. Add the garlic, ginger and coriander stalks to the pan and cook for another couple of minutes. Now add the sweet potato and mustard seeds and cook, stirring often, for a few more minutes.

Stir in the tomatoes, coconut milk, tamarind paste, lime juice and brown sugar. Bring to a simmer, then cook for 30 minutes or until the sweet potato is tender. Check and adjust the flavour.

Serve with the coriander leaves and steamed brown rice. Store in the fridge for up to a week, or freeze.

SERVES 4–6

Weekend in the country

Friday night: *Anna's minestrone ~ Alice's garlic bread*

Saturday breakfast: *Baked butterbeans with fried eggs and/or Baked apple porridge*

Saturday lunch: *Chops and sausages with Pearl barley, beetroot and yoghurt salad (page 182)*

Saturday dinner: *Braised fennel and tomato ~ Light and crunchy winter salad ~ Rich lasagne with winter greens Ginger and pear pudding with Salted caramel sauce (page 194) and ice cream*

Sunday breakfast: *Fluffy pancakes with Poached quinces (page 199) and Sweet dukkah (page 134)*

Winter weekends away with friends or at home with a houseful of visitors are my favourite. And here's why: most of our catch-ups these days seem to be on borrowed time – a quick coffee with a friend before work, half an hour for lunch to swap news and stories in rapid fire or, if we're lucky, a long lunch or dinner over the weekend. So the chance to spend a whole weekend with your favourite people is extra special. As are the good chats to be had while washing up, out for a Saturday morning walk, over a card game or during a car trip. So please, once a year if you can, beg, borrow, steal or rent a house with a group of buddies, get them all to commit to a weekend in winter and lock it in. A week out, delegate a meal per person. People are always happy to contribute if there's a team leader who's happy to delegate and make sure that not everyone brings lasagne.

My second suggestion for a great weekend away is to get some games happening. My friends think I'm a total games tragic – I walk into a room of people relaxing by the fire and instantly feel the need to organise them into some kind of activity. Charades, gin rummy, Scrabble, celebrity head; it doesn't matter what it is, as long as there's a competition underway. And while they tease me for not letting them be, it's pretty clear once the charades start, and the laughter and noise wakes up the kids, that everyone secretly loves it.

And a third tip for good weekends away: organise an outdoor activity for Saturday afternoon – a bonfire, bushwalk, game of cricket, hide and seek, whatever. Better yet, take your lunch out for a picnic. There's nothing better than coming in, all red-faced, happily exerted and hungry from the cool fresh air, to stoke the fire, pour the red wine and heat up your lasagne.

The menu

Most of the dishes on my menu can be made before the weekend and brought along to be worked into a meal. For example, with the lasagne, someone can make the ragu during the week and bring it along with lasagne sheets and the white sauce ingredients so it's more of an assembly job on the day. The minestrone, garlic bread, pudding and quinces can all be made before the weekend and then just heated, baked and gussied up a bit before serving.

This delicious, filling soup
will keep everyone going.

ANNA'S MINESTRONE

This is the perfect winter soup – hearty, tasty, full of veggies and super healthy. The recipe comes via my friend Anna, who is an excellent cook and can always be counted on to bring the goods to any gathering.

1 bunch basil
2 Tbsp olive oil
4 rashers smoky bacon, cut into strips
2 red onions, diced
1 swede, peeled and diced
1 parsnip, peeled and diced
2 carrots, peeled and diced
2 celery stalks, diced
3 garlic cloves, finely chopped
2 x 400 g (14 oz) tins chopped tomatoes
3 cups (750 ml) chicken or vegetable stock
1 glass red wine
1 handful pearl barley
1/2 cup (100 g) risoni pasta
400 g (14 oz) tin cannellini beans, drained
1 bunch English spinach, stalks removed, shredded
Shaved parmesan cheese, to serve
Extra virgin olive oil, for drizzling

Pick the basil leaves from the stalks and set aside. Finely chop the stalks.

Heat the oil in a large saucepan over medium–high heat. Add the bacon, onion, swede, parsnip, carrot, celery, garlic and basil stalks. Reduce the heat to low and sweat the bacon and vegetables, stirring occasionally, for 15 minutes or until softened.

Add the tomatoes, stock, wine and barley to the pan and simmer for 20 minutes. Add the risoni and cannellini beans, stir well and cook for 10 minutes or until the barley and risoni are tender. Stir in the spinach and cook for a minute or so until just wilted. Season to taste.

Serve the minestrone topped with the finely chopped basil leaves, parmesan and a good drizzle of olive oil.

SERVES 8

ALICE'S GARLIC BREAD

My Alice just adores garlic bread (actually, doesn't everyone?), but especially this one. It can be prepared and left in the fridge, wrapped with foil and ready to be baked, for up to 4 days.

3 garlic cloves, peeled
100 g (3 1/2 oz) butter, softened
1 handful flat-leaf parsley, finely chopped
1/4 cup (25 g) finely grated parmesan cheese
1 baguette or loaf of nice bread

Combine the garlic, butter, parsley and parmesan with some salt and pepper in a food processor and whizz to combine, or place in a mortar and bash around with the pestle until combined.

Cut the bread into 3 cm (1 1/4 inch) slices, without cutting all the way through. Spread a little garlic butter on each slice, then spread any extra over the top of the baguette.

Tightly wrap the baguette in foil and keep in the fridge until ready to bake. When that time comes, preheat the oven to 200°C (400°F). Cook the wrapped baguette for 30 minutes, then open up the foil so the top of the baguette is exposed and cook it for another 15 minutes or until golden. Serve warm.

SERVES 4–6

BAKED BUTTERBEANS WITH FRIED EGGS

I love a breakfast picnic, especially a mid-winter one when everyone rugs up and huddles around a fire to watch the sun rise. Of course, this would also be delicious served in a cosy, warm kitchen.

2–3 Tbsp olive oil, plus extra for drizzling
200 g (7 oz) bacon, cut into small pieces
1 brown onion, diced
1 garlic clove, finely chopped
1 Tbsp soft brown sugar
1 cinnamon stick
¼ tsp ground cumin
¼ tsp mixed spice
2 x 400 g (14 oz) tins chopped tomatoes
2 Tbsp Worcestershire sauce
2 cups (380 g) dried butterbeans, soaked overnight
   in cold water, then cooked until completely tender,
   or 400 g (14 oz) tin butterbeans, rinsed and drained
1 fried egg per person
Chopped flat-leaf parsley, to serve
Chilli flakes, to serve (optional)

Preheat the oven to 160°C (320°F).

Pour 2 tablespoons of the olive oil into a heavy-based ovenproof saucepan or flameproof casserole dish. Add the bacon and cook over medium–high heat until nice and crispy. Remove with a slotted spoon and set aside.

Reduce the heat to medium–low, add a little more olive oil and cook the onion and garlic until soft and translucent, about 5 minutes. Add the sugar, spices and a good seasoning of sea salt and black pepper. Cook for a few minutes more.

Add the tomatoes, cooked bacon, ½ cup (125 ml) water (or more if you think it's looking at all dry) and the Worcestershire sauce. Bring to the boil, then stir in the butterbeans. Cover with a lid or tight-fitting layer of foil and place in the oven for 45 minutes to 1 hour or until warmed through and bubbling.

Serve topped with the fried eggs, a drizzle of olive oil, lots of chopped parsley and a few chilli flakes.

SERVES 6–8

BAKED APPLE PORRIDGE

Baked porridge is a bit of a breakfast game changer. No stirring, no burnt pots, just one big tray of goodness. Plus it feels like having dessert for breakfast. You can use any fruit you like here. I usually use tart granny smith apples, but while testing for this book I also made this with fresh strawberries and poached quinces. Both were big hits. It's also lovely served sprinkled with Sweet dukkah (page 134).

   Put this together before you go to bed and leave it in the fridge, or just throw it together before breakfast. If you're preparing it in the morning, you may need to cook it for an extra 5 to 10 minutes.

4 cooking apples, peeled and thinly sliced or grated
1½ cups (150 g) rolled oats (not instant)
1 tsp ground cinnamon
1 tsp baking powder
A pinch of salt
¼ cup (45 g) soft brown sugar
⅓ cup (40 g) toasted walnuts, hazelnuts or almonds,
   roughly chopped
2 eggs
4 cups (1 litre) full-cream milk
1 tsp vanilla bean paste
Plain yoghurt and honey, to serve

Preheat the oven to 180°C (350°F). Lightly grease a 6 cup (1.5 litre) ovenproof dish. Spread the apple over the base of the dish.

Combine the oats with the cinnamon, baking powder, salt, sugar and nuts, then sprinkle the mixture over the apple.

Whisk the eggs, milk and vanilla bean paste together and pour over the oat mixture. Cover and place in the fridge overnight.

Bake for 1 hour or until the top is turning golden and the porridge is still slightly wobbly in the middle. Serve with yoghurt and a drizzle of honey.

SERVES 6–8

BRAISED FENNEL AND TOMATO

A gorgeous, easy wintery dish, this recipe can be taken in all sorts of directions. Serve it as a side dish with the lasagne and winter salad as I've suggested, or as a main meal on soft polenta with a green salad. Try it tossed through pasta or spooned over toasted sourdough and topped with a crumble of feta cheese.

¼ cup (60 ml) olive oil
6 fennel bulbs, trimmed and
 cut into quarters
2 brown onions, diced
3 garlic cloves, finely chopped
6 anchovy fillets, roughly chopped
¼ cup (45 g) green olives, pitted
 and roughly chopped
1 cup (250 ml) white wine
2 x 400 g (14 oz) tins whole peeled
 tomatoes, or 800 g (1 lb 12 oz) ripe,
 fresh tomatoes, cut into quarters
¼ cup (45 g) capers, rinsed
1 handful flat-leaf parsley leaves

Heat half the olive oil in a large heavy-based saucepan over medium–high heat. Add the fennel quarters, in batches if necessary, and cook until browned on all sides. Remove from the pan and set aside.

Reduce the heat a little and add the remaining olive oil. Cook the onion for 10 minutes or until soft and translucent. Add the garlic, anchovies and olives and cook, stirring often, for a few more minutes. Pour in the wine and cook, stirring often, until reduced by half.

Return the fennel quarters to the pan, add the tomatoes and capers and simmer for 40 minutes. Serve sprinkled with the parsley.

SERVES 8 (AS A SIDE DISH)

LIGHT AND CRUNCHY WINTER SALAD

The idea here is to offer a fresh, crunchy alternative to the richer mains on offer, so chop up a few baby cos lettuce heads and toss with some sliced radishes, cucumbers and snow peas. Crumble some feta cheese over the top and dress with a drizzle of olive oil and a splash or two of white wine vinegar. Sprinkle with some crushed up Roasted fennel and chilli nuts (page 239).

RICH LASAGNE WITH WINTER GREENS

This lasagne is a bit of a labour of love, but well worth it. And for bonus points, it contains a good serve of greens. This recipe makes either one very large lasagne – I use an enamel lasagne tray that measures 25 x 38 x 7 cm (10 x 15 x 2¾ inches) – or two smaller ones. Please consider doubling the recipe and making two large or four small lasagnes.

THERE ARE FOUR STEPS TO THIS RECIPE

1. Make a double batch of the Spicy, smoky beef ragu from page 35. This can (and should) be done a day or at least a few hours before you want to assemble and bake the lasagne. Allow for about 3 hours in the oven.

2. Wilt the greens.

3. Make the white sauce (allow about 20 minutes).

4. Assemble and bake!

For the ragu
Pop over to page 35 and make a double quantity of that gorgeous, richly flavoured beef ragu.

For the greens
2 Tbsp olive oil
1 brown onion, diced
8 cups (about 450 g) mixed shredded greens
 (kale, English spinach and chard are all good)
A pinch of salt
A pinch of freshly ground black pepper

Heat the oil in a saucepan over medium–high heat. Cook the onion for about 5 minutes or until soft and translucent. Add the greens a few handfuls at a time, adding the salt and pepper as you go, and stirring so the greens wilt and allow room for more. Continue adding the greens and cook until they are just wilted. Set aside in the pan until assembly time.

For the white sauce
80 g (2¾ oz) butter
⅔ cup (100 g) plain flour
4 cups (1 litre) milk, warmed
A pinch of freshly grated nutmeg
½ cup (50 g) grated parmesan cheese

Melt the butter in a saucepan over medium heat. Once it's bubbling, add the flour and cook for a few minutes, whisking all the time, until you have a thick paste. Add a ladleful of milk and whisk until smooth. Add a few more ladlefuls of milk, whisking until smooth. Continue until all of the milk has been incorporated. Cook, whisking often, for 5 minutes or until you have a smooth, thick sauce. Remove from the heat and whisk in the nutmeg and parmesan.

To assemble
350 g (12 oz) instant lasagne sheets
200 g (7 oz) mozzarella cheese, torn into small pieces
1 cup (100 g) grated parmesan cheese

Preheat the oven to 180°C (350°F).

Spread a third of the ragu over the base of a lasagne dish. Top with a layer of lasagne sheets, then a third of the white sauce and sprinkle with a third of the mozzarella and parmesan. Add half of the greens, then top with another third of the ragu. Top with some more lasagne sheets and another third of the white sauce and cheeses. Add the remaining greens and then the remaining ragu. Top with a final layer of lasagne sheets and the remaining white sauce.

Finish with the remaining cheeses and pop into the oven to cook for 40 minutes (or cover well and place in the fridge or freezer until needed).

NOTE
It's important that the ragu is only reheated once after it's cooked. If you're making this as a helpful present, assemble the lasagne but don't bake it – just include a note with the baking instructions.

SERVES 8–10

GINGER AND PEAR PUDDING

A classic and for good reason – this pudding can be made in advance, then warmed up when it's time for dessert. It's super delicious, comforting and easy to make. Serve it with Salted caramel sauce (page 194), gently warmed in a small saucepan over medium heat.

1 cup (160 g) pitted dates
1/2 cup (110 g) crystallised ginger
1 tsp bicarbonate of soda
1 1/2 cups (375 ml) boiling water
80 g (2 3/4 oz) butter, softened
3/4 cup (165 g) firmly packed soft
    brown sugar
2 eggs
1 tsp vanilla bean paste
1 1/2 cups (225 g) plain flour
1 tsp baking powder
1 tsp ground ginger
1/2 tsp ground cinnamon
3 pears, thinly sliced
Salted caramel sauce (page 194),
    to serve
Vanilla ice cream, to serve

Preheat the oven to 160°C (320°F). Grease and line a 25 cm (10 inch) round cake tin with baking paper.

Combine the dates, crystallised ginger and bicarbonate of soda in the bowl of your food processor and pour in the boiling water. Set aside for a few minutes.

Add the butter, sugar, eggs and vanilla to the food processor and whizz everything together for a few seconds. Now add the flour, baking powder and spices and whizz again so you have a smooth batter.

Pour the batter into the cake tin and top with the pear slices. Bake for 45 minutes or until the centre of the pudding feels springy and it is just starting to pull away from the side of the tin.

Serve the pudding warm, with the warm caramel sauce and a scoop or two of vanilla ice cream.

SERVES 8

End the day on a sweet note with this pudding – then a game of cards.

FLUFFY PANCAKES

Orange-based photographer and friend Pip Farquharson made these pancakes for breakfast at a workshop I co-hosted recently and they were a big fat hit. Fluffy, sweet and really the best way to start a lazy Sunday morning, don't you think?

3 eggs
2 Tbsp caster sugar
1 1/3 cups (200 g) self-raising flour
150 ml (5 fl oz) milk
50 g (1 3/4 oz) butter
Plain yoghurt, to serve
Sweet dukkah (page 134), to serve
Poached quinces, to serve (follow the method used in the Quince butter recipe on page 199)

Whisk the eggs and sugar until light and fluffy, then fold in the flour, followed by the milk. Gently mix together until well combined.

Heat a knob of butter in a non-stick frying pan over medium heat. Drop a good dollop of the batter into the pan, cook for a few minutes until bubbles appear, then gently flip over to cook for another couple of minutes. Repeat with the remaining batter, cooking two or three at a time (depending on the size of your frying pan).

I've served these with a dollop of plain yoghurt, a good sprinkle of dukkah and some warm poached quinces on the side and they are DELICIOUS. Any of the following seasonal options would be lovely too:

~ Rhubarb compote (page 30) and toasted, crushed hazelnuts
~ Fresh berries
~ Sliced bananas, honey and toasted, crushed pecans
~ Fresh honeycomb and orange segments
~ Roasted vanilla strawberries with a little whipped cream or coconut cream.

SERVES 6

A tray in bed

Aromatic chicken pho ~ Ginger, lemon and turmeric super tonic ~ Spoonful of sunshine orange jelly

I remember one of the only good things about feeling sick when we were kids
was that Mum let us eat dinner on a tray in bed. It seemed like such a treat to be allowed
to eat in bed and have everything plated up and delivered as if we were some kind of
very important person. There's something pretty lovely about having a tray of
good things delivered bedside when you're feeling poorly, so here are a few options
that you might like to make, deliver and administer next time one of your
people is laid low with the flu or similar.

There's something lovely about having a tray delivered bedside when you're feeling poorly.

AROMATIC CHICKEN PHO

Since last year when we visited Vietnam as a family, this recipe has become our go-to chicken soup recipe, especially when people are feeling lacklustre. I don't for a second pretend that this is an authentic pho, rather our take on the concept of chicken cooked in an aromatic broth, served with noodles and herbs. It's clean and light, yet the broth is loaded with flavour.

There is a bit of time involved in this recipe, but ninety per cent of it is hands off and the result is one hundred per cent worth it.

3 brown onions, roughly chopped
4 garlic cloves, halved
4 cm (1½ inch) piece ginger, roughly chopped
3 cinnamon sticks
4 star anise
1 whole chicken, about 1.5 kg (3 lb 5 oz)
⅓ cup (80 ml) fish sauce
⅓ cup (80 ml) soy sauce
1 Tbsp soft brown sugar
200 g (7 oz) rice vermicelli noodles
2 cups (230 g) bean sprouts
1 handful mint leaves
1 handful basil leaves
1 lime, quartered
1 fresh red chilli, finely chopped

Preheat the oven to 200°C (400°F). Line a baking tray with baking paper. Put the chopped onion, garlic and ginger on the tray and roast for 30 minutes or until beginning to crisp up. Add the cinnamon and star anise and cook for a further 10 minutes.

Put the chicken in a large stockpot with the roasted onion, garlic, ginger and spices. Add the fish sauce, soy sauce, sugar and enough water to cover the chicken. Bring to the boil over high heat, then reduce the heat to a simmer and cook for 1 hour or until the chicken is cooked through.

Remove the chicken from the stockpot. Strain the stock, discarding the aromatics, then return the stock to the pot. Check and adjust the seasoning – does it need more salt, sweetness or tang?

Once the chicken is cool enough to handle, shred the meat and pop it in a container in the fridge. Return the skin and bones to the stockpot and cook over medium–high heat for a further 1 hour. At this point you can either strain the stock into a container and chill or freeze it, or continue preparing your pho.

Cook the noodles according to the packet instructions, then rinse and divide among four to six bowls. Arrange the bean sprouts and herbs in a serving bowl, and the lime wedges and chilli in another bowl.

Place some of the shredded chicken on top of each pile of noodles and then ladle over the hot chicken stock. Let everyone add their own herbs and other flavourings.

SERVES 4–6

GINGER, LEMON AND TURMERIC SUPER TONIC

I call this a super tonic purely because it tastes super and like a tonic. A shot of this a couple of times a day when you have a cold, are trying to avoid a cold or are on the cusp of one, does seem to help. Make a double batch, keep one for your fridge and give a jar to a sniffly friend.

½ cup (around 80 g) roughly chopped fresh ginger
  (I scrub it but don't bother with peeling)
¼ cup (around 30 g) fresh turmeric, roughly
  chopped (see Note)
½ tsp freshly ground black pepper
Juice of 4 lemons
A pinch of cayenne pepper (optional)

Combine all the ingredients in a blender, add ½ cup (125 ml) water and whizz until you have the smoothest paste possible. Add 1 cup (250 ml) water and whizz again. Strain the mixture through a sieve lined with muslin if you like, but I don't mind a bit of texture in this tonic so don't bother. Keep it in the fridge for up to 2 weeks.

To serve, just knock the tonic back as a shot, straight from the fridge, or dilute it with hot water, sweeten with a little honey and sip like a tea.

NOTE
I've seen fresh turmeric popping up at supermarkets, but if it's not at yours, either use 3 teaspoons turmeric paste, or swap it for 2 tablespoons ground turmeric.

MAKES ABOUT 2 CUPS

SPOONFUL OF SUNSHINE ORANGE JELLY

A little pot of cold orange jelly is exactly what I'd like someone to make me next time I'm laid low with the flu or just a miserable cold. Like a little dose of clean sunshine, jelly is a sickbed must – refreshing, tasty, easy to swallow and digest, plus this one is full of vitamin C.

You can posh this up if you like and serve it for dessert with lightly whipped vanilla-flavoured cream and a few thin Brunekager biscuits (page 107).

4 cups (1 litre) freshly squeezed orange juice
6 gold-strength gelatine leaves
Juice of 1 lemon (optional – I like the extra tang
  this gives but if your oranges are tangy enough,
  leave it out)
1 Tbsp caster sugar, or to taste

Pour 1 cup (250 ml) of the orange juice into a shallow bowl. Add the gelatine leaves and set aside to soak.

Meanwhile, combine the rest of the orange juice with the lemon juice in a small saucepan. Bring to the boil, then remove from the heat and stir in the sugar. Taste for sweetness, adding more sugar if you like. Pour the cold juice and soaked gelatine leaves into the hot juice and whisk until the gelatine has completely dissolved.

Pour the mixture into a jelly mould, bowl or serving glasses, cover and place in the fridge to set, which usually takes about 3–4 hours.

SERVES 4

A pot of cold orange jelly is perfect sick-bed food.

Love bombs

Twice-baked goat's cheese soufflé with apples and almonds ~ Slow-cooked spiced lamb shanks
Chocolate-covered salted caramels ~ Roasted fennel and chilli nuts

Sometimes tragedy just sneaks up on you. A thing happens that makes no sense and makes you feel sick and shocked and bleak. Of course, at times like those, lamb shanks aren't the answer. There is no answer. But people still have to eat, children still need their dinner, and pantries and fridges still need to be stocked.

When grief is at high tide and those everyday needs are forgotten by the affected, it's time for us friends and family to step in. It might be with a tray of lamb shanks ready to heat and serve, or a batch of pre-cooked soufflés that ask for just a dousing in cream and a quick spell in the oven. It might be a grocery shop (and unpack), or you might even let yourself in while they're out and do a quick vacuum, throw a load of washing on and hang out or bring in and fold another. Someone did this for me once and I will never forget it. (Obviously this is only recommended when you actually know the person and are preferably related by blood or years of friendship.)

A lovely lady told me that she and her bestie have a 'love bomb' arrangement for tough times. Whenever the proverbial so-and-so hits the fan, they make dinner, cake, a jar of biscuits or whatever, and leave it at the door, sending a text before driving away that says 'incoming love bomb'. There's no pressure to answer the door, make conversation and pretend everything is okay, just a recognition that things are hard, and a clear message of support and love with no strings attached. Bombs away.

These will fill your kitchen with
the most comforting smells ever.

TWICE-BAKED GOAT'S CHEESE SOUFFLÉ WITH APPLES AND ALMONDS

The base of this recipe leans heavily on the one offered in Stephanie Alexander's bible, *The Cook's Companion*. Mum gave me this book when I moved into my first university share house, and I have been cooking from it ever since.

There is so much to love about this dish. Firstly, it is just delicious. Secondly, it can be made completely in advance, even days ahead, then doused in cream and reheated for 15 minutes before serving. And thirdly, the topping of apples and toasted almonds adds texture and brightness that cut effortlessly through the richness. You could cook these as individual soufflés or as one large one, in which case use a 6 cup (1.5 litre) ovenproof dish, then turn the soufflés out onto a larger tray before dousing them in cream.

80 g (2¾ oz) butter
⅓ cup (50 g) plain flour
1⅔ cups (420 ml) full-cream milk, warmed
A good pinch of sea salt
3 eggs, separated
1 tsp thyme leaves
¾ cup (80 g) finely grated parmesan cheese
¾ cup (90 g) crumbled goat's cheese
2 cups (500 ml) single (pure) cream
2 granny smith apples
½ cup (65 g) slivered almonds

Preheat the oven to 180°C (350°F). Melt the butter in a saucepan over medium–high heat. Dig out six 1 cup (250 ml) moulds or tea cups and brush with a little of the melted butter.

Add the flour to the remaining butter in the saucepan and cook, stirring often, for a few minutes. Pour in the milk, a little at a time, whisking after each addition so you have a thick sauce. Once all the milk is incorporated, cook, stirring often, for 5 more minutes. Remove from the heat, stir in the salt and set aside to cool for a few minutes while you whisk the egg whites until soft peaks form.

Whisk the egg yolks into the milk mixture, then add the thyme, ½ cup (50 g) of the parmesan and all of the goat's cheese. Whisk until smooth, then very, very gently fold in the egg whites.

Divide the mixture among the buttered moulds. Place the moulds in a large roasting tin and pour in boiling water to come three-quarters of the way up the sides of the moulds. Bake for 20 minutes or until the soufflés are puffed and golden. Remove from the water bath and let cool in the moulds for a few minutes before turning out into a greased gratin dish or ovenproof dish. (It doesn't really matter which way up you place the soufflés in the dish.) At this point, you can cover the dish with plastic wrap and pop it in the fridge for up to a day or two. Or you can power on for the second baking.

Pour the cream over the soufflés in the dish, sprinkle with the remaining parmesan and bake for 15 minutes or until golden and puffed up again.

While the soufflés are cooking, slice the apples into matchsticks and toast the almonds.

Top each soufflé with some of the apple and toasted almonds. Serve with a bitter green salad and some bread to mop up the creamy sauce.

SERVES 6

SLOW-COOKED SPICED LAMB SHANKS

Oh, the goodness of these lamb shanks on a cold evening! Correction: oh, the goodness of somebody making you these lamb shanks to reheat and eat on a cold evening, curled up on the couch with a blanket and some nice company (be it a person or a good movie). Make a big batch of these and enjoy them as whole shanks or shred the meat and serve as a ragu with pearl couscous. Or bake the shanks under a blanket of puff pastry, sprinkled with nigella seeds. They're are also great done in a slow cooker.

1/3 cup (80 ml) olive oil
8 lamb shanks
2 brown onions, finely diced
4 garlic cloves, finely chopped
4 cm (1 1/2 inch) piece ginger,
   finely chopped
1 bunch coriander (cilantro), stalks
   and roots finely chopped, leaves
   reserved for garnish
1 Tbsp ground cumin
1 Tbsp ground cardamom
1 Tbsp smoked paprika
1 tsp ground cinnamon
1 tsp sea salt
1 cup (250 ml) chicken or vegetable
   stock
2 x 400 g (14 oz) tins chopped
   tomatoes
8 dried figs
1/3 cup (80 ml) pomegranate molasses

Preserved lemon yoghurt
4 pieces preserved lemon rind,
   finely chopped
1/2 cup (130 g) Greek-style yoghurt

Preheat the oven to 150°C (300°F).

Heat some of the olive oil in a large heavy-based saucepan over high heat. Brown the lamb shanks, two or three at a time, for a few minutes on each side or until golden brown, adding more olive oil as necessary. Transfer all of the lamb shanks to a deep roasting tin and set aside.

Reduce the heat, add a little more oil to the pan and cook the onion, stirring often, for 10 minutes or until completely soft. Add the garlic, ginger, coriander stalks and roots, spices and salt to the pan and cook for 5 more minutes. Pour in the stock and tomatoes, then bring to the boil and cook for 5 minutes. Check and adjust the seasoning. Pour the sauce over the lamb shanks, tightly cover the roasting tin with foil and place in the oven for 3 hours or until the meat is lovely and tender. (Alternatively, transfer the lamb shanks and sauce to a slow cooker and cook on low heat for 5 hours. Add the figs and pomegranate molasses and cook for a further 1 hour.)

Remove the roasting tin from the oven and discard the foil. Tuck the dried figs among the lamb shanks and drizzle with the pomegranate molasses. Increase the heat to 180°C (350°F) and return the lamb shanks to the oven for 30 minutes.

Meanwhile, to make the preserved lemon yoghurt, simply mix the two ingredients together and season with a good grinding of black pepper.

At this point, you can either transfer the lamb shanks to a container to freeze or chill, or serve on a bed of sweet potato mash, couscous or rice. Finish with a dollop of the preserved lemon yoghurt and the reserved coriander leaves.

SERVES 8

CHOCOLATE-COVERED SALTED CARAMELS

Home-made chocolate-covered salted caramels – need I say more? Made with love, for your loved ones, they are impressive yet simple to make and always, ALWAYS well received. If you are pressed for time or if confectionery-making of any kind is just not your thing, swing by a nice chocolate shop or deli and buy a good-quality bag of chocolates, caramels or similar. These are lovely and chewy but should be kept cool so they don't go too soft. Don't forget the sprinkle of sea salt – essential.

½ cup (125 ml) single (pure) cream
110 g (3¾ oz) butter
1 cup (220 g) sugar
¼ cup (75 g) liquid glucose (or honey or golden syrup if that's what you have at hand)
450 g (1 lb) milk chocolate
Sea salt flakes, for sprinkling

Before you start, measure out all the ingredients and lightly oil and line a 21 x 13 cm (8¼ x 5 inch) loaf tin.

Combine the cream and butter in a small saucepan over medium–high heat. Cook, stirring often, until the butter has melted and the mixture reaches boiling point (don't let it boil and bubble over the pan – that's messy and annoying for you). Set aside.

Now combine ¼ cup (60 ml) water with the sugar and liquid glucose in another saucepan over medium–high heat. Try not to let the sugar splash up the side of the pan or it may crystallise later on and make the caramels grainy. Heat to boiling point and, using a pastry brush dipped in water, give the side of the saucepan a little brush to ensure no sugar crystals are lurking. Pop a sugar thermometer into the pan and cook until the mixture reaches 173°C (343°F) – it will turn a lovely amber colour. At this point, pour in the hot cream mixture in a slow, steady stream and use the thermometer to stir the mixture together. Be careful as it will all bubble up like crazy. Return the thermometer to the side of the saucepan and cook again until the mixture reaches 118°C (244°F).

Pour the caramel into the loaf tin and place in the fridge to firm up for at least 2 hours. It should be firm enough to cut at this point. Turn out onto a board and cut into even squares or bars. Place these on a tray lined with baking paper so they are sitting a little apart.

Melt the chocolate in a bowl over a saucepan of simmering water. Using two forks, dip a piece of caramel into the chocolate and swirl it around so it is completely covered, then return to the tray and sprinkle with sea salt. (You could just get a fork and dip it into the melted chocolate, then drizzle it over the caramels – this is a much easier approach and while it doesn't give a completely covered caramel, it also looks and tastes great.) Repeat with the remaining caramels. Store in the fridge.

MAKES ABOUT 20

ROASTED FENNEL AND CHILLI NUTS

These are a total winner, very more-ish and great to send someone for a little thank you or similar. They are also fabulous bashed up a bit and sprinkled over salads, such as Pearl barley, beetroot and yoghurt salad (page 182). You could even post them, but do so in a plastic container or bag inside a box. Glass jars are pretty but breakable!

Vegetable oil, for greasing
¼ cup (55 g) caster sugar
1 Tbsp sea salt
1 tsp ground chilli or chilli flakes
1 Tbsp fennel seeds
2 egg whites
4 cups (about 560 g) nuts (I went with almonds and walnuts, but you could substitute cashews, macadamias, pecans, etc.)

Preheat the oven to 150°C (300°F). Rub a large baking tray with a little vegetable oil.

Put the sugar, salt, chilli and fennel seeds in a small bowl and mix well.

In a separate, larger bowl, whisk the egg whites until frothy. Add the nuts and the sugar mixture to the egg whites and gently fold to combine.

Spread the nut mixture over the tray and pop in the oven for 40 minutes, mixing everything around halfway through. Turn off the oven but leave the tray in there to cool (scrape the mixture off the bottom of the tray after about 10 minutes to make sure it doesn't stick while cooling). Store the nuts in a jar or airtight container.

MAKES ABOUT 4 CUPS

When life gives you lemons

Sour citrus rinds ~ Ruby grapefruit, orange and barley cordial
Lemon and passionfruit curd ~ Citrus simmer pots

Eating seasonally makes extra sense in the middle of winter when citrus fruits are
at their best and bursting with bright, tangy juice and cold-busting vitamin C. If you're
lucky enough to have a lemon, orange or lime tree (or have access to one), stock up
and get squeezing. Freeze the juice in ice-cube trays so you can have
juicy times and make these recipes all year round.

SOUR CITRUS RINDS

These are a home-made, far superior version of those horrible but weirdly addictive sour worm sweets you buy in packets from the petrol station on road trips. They aren't for everyone, though – my daughter and I LOVE them but my husband and son think they're horrible. If you like really sour sweets and flavours, these are for you.

4 oranges, 2 limes, 2 lemons and 2 pink grapefruit
    (or any other combination of citrus fruits you fancy,
    so you have about 10 pieces in total)
2½ cups (550 g) caster sugar
2 Tbsp citric acid

Halve the citrus fruits and gently scrape out the flesh. (Reserve the flesh for juice or the curd on page 244.) Cut the rind halves into 1 cm (½ inch) thick strips.

Fill a saucepan with water and bring to the boil. Add the rinds and boil for 10 minutes. Drain, then fill the saucepan with fresh water and bring to the boil again. Return the rinds to the pan to boil for 10 minutes.

Drain the rinds and return them to the empty pan with 2 cups (440 g) of the sugar and 3 cups (750 ml) water. Bring to the boil and cook for 30 minutes, then drain. Arrange the rinds on a rack set over a baking tray lined with baking paper. Place in the fridge until completely cool.

Combine the citric acid and remaining sugar in a large bowl. Toss the rinds in the sugar, then return to the drying rack, reserving the sugar, and leave at room temperature for 30 minutes (make sure you keep them away from ants). Toss the rinds in the sugar one more time, then return to the rack to dry out overnight, or for at least 8 hours. Once completely dry, store the rinds in an airtight container.

NOTE
Don't be tempted to put these in a low oven to dry out like I did: sticky city.

MAKES ABOUT 2 CUPS

RUBY GRAPEFRUIT, ORANGE AND BARLEY CORDIAL

This is just gorgeous with mineral water, ice and a slice of lemon or orange. Or mix it with boiling water and serve as a lovely warm drink.

1¼ cups (250 g) pearl barley
1¼ cups (310 ml) freshly squeezed ruby
    grapefruit juice
1¼ cups (310 ml) freshly squeezed orange juice
3 cups (660 g) sugar
¾ cup (250 g) honey
1 vanilla bean, split lengthways

Toast the barley in a large saucepan over medium–high heat, stirring often so the grains don't burn, for 5 minutes or until it turns a lovely golden colour.

Stir in the remaining ingredients and 4 cups (1 litre) water. Bring to the boil, then reduce the heat and simmer for 10 minutes. Leave to cool for 5 minutes, then strain the cordial into jars. Store in the fridge for up to 2 weeks.

MAKES ABOUT 3 CUPS

LEMON AND PASSIONFRUIT CURD

This is a lovely curd recipe: it uses whole eggs, which is nice and neat, sets well and tastes gorgeous. What it does ask for is a little time, so please keep the heat low, stir almost constantly and watch carefully. The quantities given here make quite a lot of curd but I think if you are going to spend 15 minutes stirring, you may as well get a good few jars for your trouble. If you prefer to make just lemon curd, leave out the passionfruit and add one more lemon.

220 g (7¾ oz) unsalted butter
1⅔ cups (370 g) caster sugar
Grated zest and juice of 4 lemons –
   you need ¾ cup (185 ml) juice
6 eggs, lightly beaten
½ cup (125 g) passionfruit pulp
   (you'll need about 4 passionfruit)

Put the butter, sugar and lemon zest in a glass bowl resting over a saucepan of simmering water. Cook, stirring often, until the butter has melted and the sugar has dissolved, about 5 minutes.

Add the eggs, lemon juice and passionfruit pulp and cook, gently whisking, for 15–20 minutes or until the mixture has thickened and coats the back of a wooden spoon – if you have a sugar thermometer, setting point will be around 160°C (320°F). Spoon into clean jars, seal and keep in the fridge for up to 2 weeks.

MAKES ABOUT 5 CUPS

THINGS TO DO WITH CURD

~ Make mini sweet pastry tart shells using the recipe on page 102 (or use store-bought tart shells), fill with curd and top with a dollop of thick or whipped cream.
~ Slice the Triple-ginger loaf (page 164) horizontally into thirds, spread one third with lemon curd and another third with whipped cream, then gently sandwich back together.
~ Make the Fluffy pancakes from page 224 and serve with Poached quinces (page 199) and a dollop of curd.
~ Make the Jam pastries on page 51 but fill with curd instead of jam.
~ Make the Meringues on page 98 and serve with whipped cream and curd.

OTHER CURD FLAVOURS

~ Orange curd
~ Blood orange curd
~ Lime curd
~ Raspberry curd – blitz 1 cup
(125 g) raspberries, push through
a sieve and then fold through the
cooled curd.

CITRUS SIMMER POTS

A bright, clean aroma in the kitchen can make a world of difference to your mood, so, instead of forking out for a scented candle, air freshener or burning incense, consider one of these simmer pots. They cost next to nothing, are completely natural and put much-needed moisture back into the air (especially welcome when you have the fire or heater going constantly).

Simply place the ingredients for your chosen simmer pot in a small saucepan, cover with water (it should come about three-quarters of the way up the side of the pan) and simmer, topping up the water as needed, for a few hours.

To make these up as a gift, combine all the ingredients in a jar or cellophane bag and pop in a little instruction card.

LEMON, ROSEMARY AND VANILLA

1 lemon, thinly sliced
2 rosemary sprigs
1 vanilla bean, split lengthways (scrape the seeds into the water and add the vanilla bean as well)

GRAPEFRUIT AND EUCALYPTUS

Peel of 1 grapefruit, cut into wide strips
5–6 eucalyptus leaves (crush the leaves before adding them to the pan to release their oils)

MANDARIN AND LAVENDER

Peel of 1 mandarin, cut into wide strips
3 fresh or dried lavender flower heads

SPICED ORANGE

Peel of 1 orange, cut into wide strips
2 bay leaves
2 cinnamon sticks
2 cloves
1 nutmeg

The aroma of these simmer pots will brighten both your room and your mood.

Sweet winter afternoons

Basic sweet dough ~ Sweet wreath with blood orange curd
Hot chocolate ~ Milk buns ~ Cinnamon scrolls ~ Cultured butter

For me, baking with soft, buttery yeasted doughs is the sweetest of meditations.
The basic dough on the page opposite feels so good to knead, plait and shape, and it
yields the most delicious, comforting buns, scrolls and wreaths. And then there's the
ritual of resting the dough, gently shaping it, resting again, brushing with egg wash,
sprinkling with sugar or dusting with cinnamon. If you haven't done much baking
with yeast, please start here and hopefully you'll see what I mean!

BASIC SWEET DOUGH

This is one of my favourite recipes. The dough is silky smooth and lovely to work with, and it can be made into many delightful forms, including the Mini spiced Christmas wreaths (page 108) and a large twisted wreath (see over). The sweet little Milk buns with Hot chocolate are hard to resist, as are the classic Cinnamon scrolls.

1 cup (250 ml) milk
100 g (3½ oz) butter
3 tsp dried yeast
¼ cup (55 g) caster sugar
1 egg
3⅓ cups (500 g) plain flour,
  plus extra for dusting
A pinch of salt

Combine the milk and butter in a small saucepan. Heat, stirring, until the milk is warm and the butter has melted. Remove from the heat and set aside to cool until lukewarm.

Tip the milk and butter mixture into the bowl of an electric mixer with a dough attachment.

Add the yeast, sugar, egg, flour and salt and knead for 5 minutes. Turn out onto a lightly floured work surface and finish kneading by hand for a minute or so. (You can do the entire kneading process by hand if you prefer – combine the dry ingredients on a work surface, make a well in the centre and then add the milk and butter mixture and the egg, and knead together.)

Place the dough in a lightly oiled bowl, cover with a tea towel and leave in a warm place for 1 hour or until doubled in size.

SWEET WREATH WITH BLOOD ORANGE CURD

This wreath is a larger, wintery version of the mini cinnamon ones from the Christmas baking section (page 108). It's a really lovely recipe to bake and share on a cold winter's afternoon. For the curd, follow the recipe for Lemon and passionfruit curd on page 244, but swap two of the lemons with blood oranges.

Serve the wreath warm with Rhubarb compote (page 30) and a little thick cream or just a little extra blood orange curd.

1 quantity basic sweet dough
 (page 249)
Grated zest of 2 oranges
1 cup (250 ml) blood orange curd
1 Tbsp single (pure) cream
1 egg
Icing sugar, for dusting

Make the dough according to the recipe, adding the orange zest with the flour and other dry ingredients before kneading.

Once the dough has risen, gently turn it out onto a lightly floured work surface. Roll the dough into a large rectangle, then transfer to a baking tray lined with baking paper, cover with plastic wrap and place in the fridge for 1 hour. This will make the twisting part much easier.

Preheat the oven to 200°C (400°F).

Spread the dough with the blood orange curd. Roll the dough from the longest edge into a long sausage, then cut it in half lengthways to make two long half-cylinders. Place the halves next to each other, cut sides up, and twist together into a braid, pressing the ends together. This can take a bit of practice but it's fun and isn't tricky once you get the idea.

Whisk the cream and egg together to make an egg wash. Gently transfer the wreath to the lined baking tray and brush with the egg wash. Bake for 10 minutes, then reduce the heat to 180°C (350°F) and bake for a further 25 minutes or until the wreath is golden brown. Serve warm, dusted with icing sugar.

SERVES 8

This is delicious warm from the oven with a little extra blood orange curd.

HOT CHOCOLATE

Pour 1 cup (250 ml) milk per person into a saucepan. Warm over medium heat until just boiling. Remove the pan from the heat and stir in $^1/_4$ cup (35 g) roughly chopped chocolate per person (I use milk chocolate for the kids and a nice dark chocolate for me).

MILK BUNS

My maternal grandfather was Danish and my fondest memory of visiting Copenhagen was arriving at our hotel on a cold-to-the-bone afternoon to find a tray of warm milk buns set up in a cosy, fire-lit corner of the lobby. With the buns was a jug of hot chocolate, a bowl of cream and a smaller bowl of chocolate coffee beans. Heaven.

I can't think of a more comforting thing to make and deliver to a friend or family who are having a difficult time. Children in particular adore this combination. Serve the buns warm (or reheated) within a day or two of baking.

1 quantity basic sweet dough (page 249)
2 tsp ground cardamom
1 egg
2 Tbsp single (pure) cream
1/3 cup (75 g) caster sugar

Make the dough according to the recipe, adding the cardamom with the flour and other dry ingredients before kneading.

Once the dough has risen, turn it out onto a lightly floured work surface and give it a light knead. Cut the dough into 10 equal pieces and shape into neat balls. Place on a baking tray lined with baking paper and leave to rise again for 30 minutes.

Preheat the oven to 200°C (400°F). Whisk the egg and cream together and gently brush over the buns. Sprinkle with the sugar and bake for 15–20 minutes or until risen and golden. Serve the buns warm with hot chocolate.

MAKES 10

CINNAMON SCROLLS

The smell of these baking in the oven is balm for the senses – cinnamon scrolls are like a bear hug, in food form. And like any yeasted baking project, the satisfaction value when pulling these golden beauties out of the oven is off the charts.

1 quantity basic sweet dough (page 249)
100 g (3 1/2 oz) butter, softened
1/2 cup (110 g) firmly packed soft brown sugar
1 Tbsp ground cinnamon
1 egg
1 Tbsp single (pure) cream

Roll the dough out on a lightly floured work surface into a rectangle, about 35 x 25 cm (14 x 10 inches).

Put the butter, brown sugar and cinnamon in a bowl and mix until well combined. Spread the butter over the dough (I usually start with the back of a spoon and then use my fingers to spread it to cover the whole rectangle).

Gently roll the dough from the longest edge of the rectangle into a long sausage. Cut the sausage into 4 cm (1 1/2 inch) pieces and place on a lined baking tray, swirly side up, leaving 1 cm (1/2 inch) between each one so they can spread as they cook. Leave to rise for about 30 minutes.

Preheat the oven to 200°C (400°F). Whisk the egg and cream together to make an egg wash. Brush the rolls with the egg wash, then cook in the oven for 20 minutes or until golden.

MAKES ABOUT 12

CULTURED BUTTER

So easy, so delicious and so impressive, home-made cultured butter is completely different to what you buy in the shops. Plus, you end up not only with fresh, delicious butter but also a bottle of home-made buttermilk to bake with or use in the Buttermilk soup on page 133.
Check the label of the cream to ensure it contains no thickeners or preservatives – a good non-homogenised cream is ideal, otherwise a carton of thin, pure cream will be fine.

4 cups (1 litre) single (pure) cream
1/2 cup (130 g) Greek-style yoghurt with live cultures
1/2 tsp sea salt

You'll need a stand mixer with a whisk attachment. Combine the cream and yoghurt in the bowl, cover with plastic wrap and leave in the fridge overnight.

Place the bowl on the stand mixer and cover the top of the bowl with plastic wrap so nothing can splash out while mixing. Don't skip this step – you'll regret it when you're cleaning curd and buttermilk off the ceiling! Begin whisking, and keep going until you see the mixture separate into clumps of butter and buttermilk. Pour the buttermilk into a sterilised bottle and store it in the fridge for up to 3 days.

Bring all of the butter together in your hands and mix in the salt, then rinse under cold running water to wash away as much buttermilk as possible.

Now, you want to 'work the curds' on a clean wooden surface. This simply means rolling and working the butter between your hands to remove the moisture. Form the butter into a log shape, wrap it in baking paper and keep in the fridge for up to a week.

MAKES ABOUT 350 G (12 OZ) BUTTER

Compound butter

To really gild the lily, you could take your beautiful cultured butter and turn it into a compound butter, which is essentially flavoured butter. Below are four ideas you could try, but the options really are endless. One more idea: divide the cultured butter into four portions and flavour each as suggested below, then wrap up, label and give away with a few serving ideas. I'd love to receive that little gift; it could lead to so many good, easy meals that I might not even think of if preoccupied with life's more messy moments.

~ Truffle butter

Grate a small black truffle into the soft butter with a little sea salt, then form into a gloriously scented log.

~ Cinnamon and maple syrup butter

Mix 1 tablespoon maple syrup and 1/2 teaspoon ground cinnamon into 100 g (3 1/2 oz) soft butter. Serve spread on pancakes and waffles. Or peel and halve a few apples or pears, cut out the cores and fill with 1 tablespoon of the butter. Arrange in a roasting tin, splash a little white wine or water into the dish and roast until the fruit is completely soft.

~ Sage and orange butter

Mix 2 tablespoons finely chopped sage, the grated zest of 1 orange and a good grinding of black pepper into 100 g (3 1/2 oz) soft butter. Spread on warm dinner rolls; spoon into baked potatoes; toss with steamed green beans; or dollop on top of grilled chicken breasts.

~ Anchovy and caper butter

Mix 3 finely chopped anchovies, 3 finely chopped capers and 3 finely chopped garlic cloves into 100 g (3 1/2 oz) soft butter. Add half a handful each of finely chopped flat-leaf parsley and chives. Serve on top of an indulgent, barbecued rib-eye or scotch fillet steak or baked salmon fillet.

INDEX

ACKNOWLEDGEMENTS

This book is for Tim, Alice and Tom. Our little family is everything to me. Thank you, guys, for your love and support, and, right back at you.

As anyone whose primary income depends on primary industry knows, the farming life can be really hard. It's a juggle, a gamble and a 24 hour/7 days a week job. And yes, it's a cliche, but despite the challenges we do look around us every day and feel grateful we get to live here on this farm, in this place together. Thank you, Tim and ALL the farmers who grow and produce our food, for keeping the boat afloat through drought, bushfires, all the uncertainties and challenges.

Thank you to my parents, Annie and Henry Herron, whose beautiful property features prominently throughout this book. Thank you for giving my siblings and me confidence, opportunity and a home we always love to come back to.

Thank you to the team at Murdoch Books, especially Corinne Roberts who has guided me through this process with such skill and warmth, and designer Vivien Valk who has worked so hard to make this book so beautiful.

Big thanks to Josie Chapman for opening up her beautiful cottages at the Old Convent B&B Borenore for our cover photography.

Making and sharing good, simple, seasonal food is an act of love and generosity, so my final thanks is to you, for buying this book and hopefully taking inspiration from it to go out and leave a basket of homemade food at someone's door soon. It will mean so much to them.

Published in 2019 by Murdoch Books,
an imprint of Allen & Unwin

Murdoch Books Australia
83 Alexander Street, Crows Nest NSW 2065
Phone: +61 (0)2 8425 0100
murdochbooks.com.au
info@murdochbooks.com.au

Murdoch Books UK
Ormond House, 26–27 Boswell Street,
London, WC1N 3JZ
Phone: +44 (0) 20 8785 5995
murdochbooks.co.uk
info@murdochbooks.co.uk

For Corporate Orders & Custom Publishing
contact our business development team at
salesenquiries@murdochbooks.com.au

Publisher: Corinne Roberts
Design Manager and Designer: Vivien Valk
Editorial Manager: Jane Price
Editor: Justine Harding
Photography: Sophie Hansen, except page 249
by Lina Hayes, and cover and pages 2, 4–5, 263
and 264 by Clancy Paine
Production Director: Lou Playfair

Text and photography © Sophie Hansen
(except page 249 photograph © Lina Hayes;
cover and pages 2, 4–5, 263 and 264 © Clancy Paine)
Design © Murdoch Books 2018

ISBN 978 1 76052 362 6 Australia
ISBN 978 1 76063 459 9 UK

A cataloguing-in-publication entry is available from
the catalogue of the National Library of Australia at
nla.gov.au
A catalogue record for this book is available from the
British Library

Colour reproduction by Splitting Image Colour Studio
Pty Ltd, Clayton, Victoria
Printed by C&C Offset Printing Co Ltd, China

TABLESPOONS: We have used Australian 20 ml
(4 teaspoon) tablespoon measures. If you are using a
smaller European 15 ml (3 teaspoon) tablespoon, add
an extra teaspoon of the ingredient for each tablespoon
specified in the recipe.

MIX
Paper from
responsible sources
FSC® C008047

The paper in this book is FSC® certified.
FSC® promotes environmentally responsible,
socially beneficial and economically viable
management of the world's forests.